MEXICAN COOKING

Ruth Kershner and Josette Koch

WEATHERVANE
BOOKS

contents

introduction

Mexican cuisine is one of the oldest and most intriguing in the world. It is far older than French cuisine, from which it has borrowed. Its true origins are with the Mayan Indians, whose civilization rose and fell long before the Spaniards visited Mexico. Remnants are still apparent in today's cuisine—in the chocolate consumed by the Mexican population as a beverage and in the subtleties of Yucatanian cuisine.

The best historical references to Mexican cuisine are records kept by the Spanish conquerors of what they found in the New World. The Spaniards were welcomed into the court of the Emperor Montezuma and found great riches as well as a wealth of culture. Great feasts were served each night, composed of many dishes. All the dishes were kept warm on charcoal braziers for the guests to sample. Tortillas were made from corn flour—in many shapes and sizes. Many complicated dishes featuring wild game and elaborate sauces were served. Beans and chilies were used extensively, and many kinds were cultivated. Chocolate and fruit drinks were served to quench the thirst. Tropical fruits of many varieties were served.

The Spaniards reveled in their new-found treasures and took all these new wonders back to Europe. The conquerors took home with them corn, beans, chilies, chocolate, vanilla, tomatoes, eggplant, and potatoes.

The Spaniards also brought to the New World some very important additions to the Indian diet. While the Indians were well-known for their horticulture, they had few domesticated animals and had no readily available source of fat in the diet. The Spaniards introduced them to beef, pork (and the lard derived from it), and dairy products. While the Aztecs had bred turkeys, they had never eaten eggs, which the Spanish considered an important part of their diet.

The Indians took the new foods and assimilated them into their native diet, making a truly Creole cuisine. Today, the rice of the Spaniards is eaten mixed with native tomatoes and chilies, making a very happy marriage of flavors. In short, it was a very pleasing trade on both sides.

The short reign of the French Emperor Maximilian and the Empress Carlota brought new dimension to Mexican cuisine. Maximilian brought chefs from Austria, France, and Italy to cook for his court. The native population borrowed from the continental cuisine and added vermicelli, noodles, white continental bread, and other delicacies to the native dishes. Today, the assimilation has been so complete that chili spaghetti is made in some areas.

During World War II many Germans came to Mexico seeking refuge. They brought with them a very new and important asset. Today the beer of Mexico is recognized as some of the finest in the world, owing to the fine efforts of the German brewmeisters now living there.

There is no one cuisine or selection of foods that represents Mexico. The country is expansive in area and divided by many geographical barriers. Transportation is often poor. Many conservative Indian tribes accepted fewer of the Spanish ways, preserving more of the Indian culture and developing their own distinctive dishes based on the foods available. Thus, one dish, for example tamales, may be cooked in thousands of different ways throughout the country and still be called Mexican.

The basic foods of Aztec times still remain, even though the recipes have long been lost. Corn, beans, and chili are still the staff of life. Corn is boiled in a lime solution, husked, and boiled again to form hominy (or *pozole*), which is used in soup, or it is ground to form masa, from which tortillas are made. The dough is also used to make tamales, to thicken sauces, and as the basis of a gruel-like beverage known as atole. Many varieties of beans are grown. They range in color from pink, to tan, to black and brown, the darker beans being preferred. They are boiled in earthenware pots and then eaten sparked with chili or mashed and fried in fat and eaten (refried beans) at almost every meal. Chilies are grown in every area of Mexico, with at least 61 different varieties now found in cultivation. Tropical fruits are always available and quite inexpensive. They are often served in place of dessert. Chicken, pork, turkey, eggs, and cheese are used frequently in the diet. Beef is used more heavily in the north of Mexico, where large plains make grazing more practical. Fish is eaten frequently in the coastal areas. Milk is available, but generally is not consumed as a beverage by adults. It is combined with chocolate or coffee or used in sweetened puddings and desserts. Fresh vegetables are available and are eaten in a variety of ways, especially as salads, popular in the warm climate. Sugar cane was introduced by the Spaniards and grows in great abundance in Mexico. Sugar is cheap, and sweets are eaten in great abundance.

A variety of alcoholic beverages also are available. The sap is drawn from the maguey cactus and fermented to form the local beverage, pulque. Unhappily, pulque does not ship well even over small distances. Therefore, the sap is fermented and distilled to form tequila, which is a popular drink in Mexico and around the world. Beer is widely available and makes an excellent accompaniment to a Mexican dinner. Fruit beverages, for example lemonade, are frequent thirst-quenchers, and it must also be noted that Coca Cola has made its inroads in Mexico.

Many ancient cooking techniques are still employed in Mexican homes. The country is basically not rich, but has a small and now growing middle class. Refrigeration is not common outside the cities. Charcoal-fired stoves and griddles are frequently used in cooking. Ovens are often heated with wood and situated out doors. For this reason, few casserole dishes are served. Soups, stews, and other stove-top dishes are served more frequently. However, certain modern changes are taking the place of old ways. Tortillerias are springing up in even the smallest villages. Machinery takes the masa dough, presses it into tortillas, bakes it, and delivers it into the waiting hands of the consumer, cutting out hours of labor. Electric blenders are now rapidly replacing the mortar and pestle in Mexican kitchens.

The Mexican meal pattern differs considerably from the traditional American one. Although there are five recognized mealtimes each day, few people can afford or desire to eat all five meals. In the morning one can have *desayuno,* or early breakfast. This generally consists of a roll and coffee or chocolate. *Almuerzo* is the American equivalent of brunch, served late in the morning and consisting of fruit, bread or tortillas, eggs and/or meat, and coffee. *Comida* is the main meal of the day and is usually eaten early in the afternoon. A formal *comida* can consist of as many as six courses. First, appetizers are served, followed by soup (*sopa seca* or dry soup—a rice dish), chicken or fish, the entree, beans served as a separate course, dessert, and coffee—all followed by a well-deserved siesta. *Merienda* at 6 P.M. serves as a sort of high tea, featuring coffee or chocolate and cakes or cookies. *Cena* (supper) is served late and is light. There is no doubt that the Mexicans like to eat, for, in addition to all these meals, vendors can be found on any corner selling *antojitos*—little whimsies that can be anything from a taco or burrito to sweet dessert or fresh fruit.

Mexican cuisine is a delicious experience and well worth trying. It requires few special supplies and only a little extra time in a modern kitchen. Even one Mexican dish livens up an ordinary meal! Try it and you will see.

guide to unusual ingredients

achiote—This is the Mexican name given to Annatto, which are the seeds of a South American tree. It has a delicate flavor and a dark reddish-orange color. It is available in jars in Latin American markets and gourmet stores. It may also be purchased ground.

beans—Commercially available dried beans of the pinto, kidney, or black-bean variety are satisfactory for the recipes in this book. Canned refried beans and beans in Mexican sauce are also available in many supermarkets.

chili peppers—As previously stated, more than 61 kinds of chili peppers are grown in Mexico. However, only a few are necessary to Mexican cooking. There are two basic classifications for these peppers: fresh or canned, and dried.

fresh or canned chili peppers

jalapeño pepper—This is a canned pickled green chili and can be found in gourmet sections of most supermarkets. It is very hot, so handle with care. Sauce containing this chili is readily available.

anaheim chilies—These are canned green chilies and are usually available labeled as peeled green chilies. If seeded, they are only slightly hot. Leave some of the seeds for more heat. They are grown in California and are widely available in the specialty sections of supermarkets. Fresh hot chilies can be substituted for these chilies, but they vary a great deal in hotness, so test before you add too many. If fresh chilies are to be added in quantity to any dish or to be stuffed, they should be roasted and peeled first. Roast them over an open flame or in the broiler until their skins blister. Wrap them in a towel to steam for a few minutes, then peel them under cold running water.

All chilies should be handled with care, as they contain a chemical irritant. Seed them carefully under cold running water. Wash your hands well afterward, and take care not to rub your eyes when working with the chilies. Use less than the amount of chili listed when first preparing a recipe. Then taste and add chili peppers or powder to suit your taste. It is easy to add more fire to a dish and impossible to take it out. Always add less chili to a dish being prepared ahead of time, as the hotness seems to increase on standing.

dried

ancho chilies—These are large, mild, sweet chilies that, when dried, are dark red to brown in color and are 2 to 3 inches long. They are usually available in the dried form only and may be stored indefinitely. They are usually found only in Latin markets. There is no substitute.

passilla and pequin chilies—These are moderately hot and very hot dried chilies, respectively. If they cannot be found, use crushed red pepper or cayenne to achieve the desired degree of hotness in a given recipe.

chili powder—Chili powder is a mixture of powdered chili peppers and spices and herbs. Buy the freshest chili powder you can get and experiment with it until you find out how hot your brand is.

chorizo—This is Mexican sausage. It can be purchased at Latin American markets, or you can try making your own from the recipe in this book (see Index).

cilantro—This is leaf coriander. It is also called Chinese parsley and is available in Oriental and Latin American grocery stores. It is available also in dried form.

comino—This is cumin seed. It is commercially available in spice sections of supermarkets. If it is whole, it must be crushed to release the flavor.

masa harina—This instant limed corn flour is used in making tortillas, tamales, and other Mexican dishes. It is often stocked in specialty sections of supermarkets, or it can be obtained at a Latin American market.

Mexican chocolate—Mexican chocolate is used to make drinks or to flavor Mexican Mole sauce. It is bitter chocolate ground with cinnamon and almonds and then sweetened with sugar. It can be obtained at Latin American markets, or you can substitute semisweet chocolate (ounce for ounce) and ½ teaspoon ground cinnamon.

Monterey Jack cheese—This is a creamy white cheese that is mild in flavor and smooth in texture. It is widely available in the United States and closely approximates mild Mexican cheese in taste. If it is not available in your area, substitute Meunster cheese.

queso blanco—Queso Blanco is a Latin American cheese. It is salty and mild to taste and is crumbly in texture. It does not melt quite as easily as Jack cheese. Latin American stores and some supermarkets sell it. Substitute Jack cheese in place of it when called for in a recipe.

pepitas—Pepitas are shelled pumpkin seeds. They are available raw or roasted and salted in snack sections of the supermarkets. Squash seeds may be substituted.

tortillas—Tortillas are thin unleavened corn cakes, baked on a comal or griddle. They are the bread of Mexico and have been eaten since Aztec times. They are available fresh in dairy sections of many markets. In the Eastern section of the United States they are also available in frozen or canned forms. Defrost frozen tortillas before using. They may then be substituted for fresh tortillas in any cooked recipe. If you live in an area where tortillas and masa flour are not available, cornmeal crepes can be used in enchilada recipes, with pleasing results. Try using homemade flour tortillas for fried items such as tacos or tostadas.

tomatillo or tomate verde—This is a very small, sweet green tomato. It is not at all like the unripe green tomato of the United States. They are available canned and are pureed whole, using part or all of the liquid from the can. There is no substitute for this ingredient.

appetizers and snacks

chili and cheese appetizers
nachos

1 dozen 6-inch corn tortillas
Oil for frying
6 pickled jalapeño peppers
   (*Jalapeño en Escabeche*)

1 cup refried beans
   (homemade or canned)
½ cup shredded sharp
   cheddar cheese

Cut each tortilla into quarters.

Heat 1 inch of oil to 360°F in a small heavy skillet. Fry tortillas until crisp; drain on paper towels.

Carefully stem and seed peppers; cut each into 6 thin strips.

Spread each chip with 1 teaspoon beans. Top with ½ teaspoon shredded cheese and a thin pepper strip. Broil until cheese melts. Serve immediately. Makes 48 appetizers.

cheddar-cheese puffs
bocadillos de queso y aceituna

2 cups grated cheddar cheese
½ cup butter or margarine,
   softened
1 cup flour, sifted
½ teaspoon salt
½ teaspoon paprika
48 small green olives, stuffed
   with pimientos

Blend cheese with butter. Add sifted flour, salt, and paprika; mix well. Mold 1 teaspoon dough around each olive to cover.

At this point you may refrigerate or freeze cheese puffs for up to 10 days.

Bake puffs at 400°F for 15 minutes. Serve hot. Makes 48 appetizers.

fiesta cheese ball
bolita de queso

8 ounces cream cheese
1 pound sharp cheddar
  . cheese, grated
¼ cup butter, softened
1 tablespoon chili powder
5 cups chopped black olives
½ cup dried parsley

Have cheeses and butter at room temperature before combining with an electric mixer.

Beat cream cheese and butter until combined. Add cheddar and chili powder. Mix well. Add olives; mix lightly. Form into 2 balls; roll balls in dried parsley. Chill well. (Cheese balls may be frozen for later use.)

Serve cheese balls with assorted crackers. Makes 2 balls.

As a variation omit the butter and chili powder and substitute 1 4-ounce can of chopped green chilies.

avocado dip
guacamole

For raw vegetables or corn chips.

3 ripe avocados
1 tomato, peeled and seeded
1 small red onion, finely diced
1 tablespoon chopped hot
  jalapeño pepper
Dash of ground coriander
1 tablespoon lemon juice
1 tablespoon vinegar
2 tablespoons salad oil
1 teaspoon salt

Mince avocados and tomato. Stir in all other ingredients; spoon into individual dishes. You may use scooped-out avocado shells for serving dishes.

If made ahead of time, put the avocado seeds in the mixture to keep it green. Makes 8 servings (2 cups).

chili and cheese dip
chili con queso

2 tablespoons olive oil
1 medium onion, finely
  chopped
1 12-ounce can tomatoes,
  drained and chopped
1 4-ounce can chopped green
  chilies
1 pound pasteurized processed
  American cheese spread

Heat oil in medium skillet; sauté onion until golden. Add tomatoes and chilies. Reduce heat to simmer; cook mixture until almost dry, stirring occasionally.

Meanwhile, melt cheese over hot water in double boiler. Combine melted cheese and tomato mixture.

Serve dip in chafing dish or fondue pot, so that dip remains warm. Serve with corn chips or tostadas. Makes 6 to 8 servings.

bean dip
aperitivo de frijoles refritos

1 1-pound can refried beans
⅓ cup hot jalapeño relish (or
   more, to taste)
Sour cream (optional)
¾ cup grated Jack cheese

Combine beans with the jalapeño relish, stirring well. If mixture is too thick, add a small amount of sour cream; mix well. Place in three ramekins; sprinkle each with ¼ cup of cheese. Heat ramekins, as needed, at 350°F for 20 minutes.

Serve dip hot with tortilla chips. Makes 6 servings, depending on the other appetizers.

hot dip
salsa cruda

1 1-pound can tomatoes,
   drained and chopped
1 cup chopped scallions
   (onions and green stem)
1 teaspoon salt
1 4-ounce can green chili
   sauce

Mix tomatoes, scallions, and salt. Add green chili sauce to taste. Chill. Makes 1 cup (8 servings).

shrimp dip
camarónes

¼ cup chili sauce
2 teaspoons lemon juice
1 teaspoon prepared
   horseradish
¼ teaspoon salt
4 drops hot-pepper sauce
1 cup sour cream
1 4½-ounce can shrimp,
   drained and chopped (1 cup
   shrimp)

Combine chili sauce, lemon juice, horseradish, salt, and hot-pepper sauce. Fold in sour cream. Add chopped shrimp. Chill.

Serve dip with crisp vegetables. Makes 8 servings (1¾ cups).

tortilla chips
totopos

1 dozen corn tortillas
Oil for frying
Salt

Defrost tortillas if they are frozen. Cut each tortilla into 8 wedges.

Use a small heavy skillet, electric skillet, or deep fryer to heat at least 1 inch of cooking oil to 360°F. Fry tortilla pieces, a few at a time, until crisp and lightly browned. Remove from oil with a slotted spoon. Drain chips on paper towels and salt lightly.

Serve chips with dips or refried beans. Makes 8 dozen chips.

tortillas and beans
burritos

Beans and cheese are only the beginning of the list of possible burrito fillings. Leftover taco filling or other ground meat, chicken, and chili sauce, or just cheese make a delicious sandwich.

4 large flour tortillas (7 to 8 inches in diameter or larger)

3 cups refried beans
½ cup grated cheddar cheese
¼ cup Green Chili Salsa

Lightly brush tortillas with water; heat briefly on griddle until warm and pliable.

Meanwhile, heat refried beans to serving temperature. Place ¾ cup beans down center of each tortilla. Top with 2 tablespoons grated cheese and 1 tablespoon Green Chili Salsa. Fold top and bottom edges of tortilla in 2 inches, then fold sides toward center, overlapping each other. At this point it is wisest to wrap a napkin around the sandwich to hold it shut. Makes 4 servings.

stuffed eggs
huevos rellenos

8 hard-cooked eggs, chilled
1 tablespoon grated onion
1 tablespoon finely minced green pepper
¼ teaspoon chili powder
¼ teaspoon salt
2 to 3 dashes Tabasco

2 teaspoons lemon juice
1 tablespoon olive oil
16 small shrimp, cooked, peeled, and deveined
Parsley
Lettuce

Cut hard-cooked eggs in half lengthwise; remove yolks. Mash yolks with onion, green pepper, chili powder, salt, Tabasco, lemon juice, and olive oil. Stuff egg whites with egg-yolk mixture; garnish each egg with a shrimp and a tiny sprig of parsley.

Place eggs on a plate surrounded by fresh green lettuce. Refrigerate until serving time. Makes 4 or more servings.

crisp-fried burritos
chimichangas

These sandwiches are a California-Mexican treat and can be filled with any filling you wish. For example: leftover taco filling, chicken and chilies, or beans. One of these makes a more than ample lunch.

4 large flour tortillas (7 to 8 inches in diameter or larger)
2 cups grated extra-sharp cheddar cheese
1 4-ounce can chopped green chilies

Oil for frying
Chili con Carne (see Index)
Chopped white onion
Grated cheddar cheese

Lay tortillas briefly on a hot griddle, to make them pliable. Fill immediately with ½ cup cheese and 1 tablespoon chilies placed in center of each tortilla. Fold top and bottom edges in toward center 1 or 2 inches, then fold sides toward center, overlapping each other to form a tight package. Fasten with a toothpick.

Heat 1 inch oil to 360°F in an electric skillet. Fry burritos until golden brown, turning once. Drain on paper towels.

Serve burritos topped with chili, onions, and grated cheese. Makes 4 servings.

cocktail meatballs
albondiguitas

Very different!

1 pound lean hamburger
1 teaspoon garlic powder
1 12-ounce bottle chili sauce
1 10-ounce jar grape jelly

Mix hamburger with garlic powder and shape into small balls. Pan fry until well-cooked; drain.

Mix chili sauce and grape jelly. Add meatballs; heat mixture.

Serve sauce warm in chafing dish. Makes 12 servings as an appetizer.

shrimp appetizer-cocktail
aperitivo de camarónes

1 pound fresh large shrimp, in the shell
1 head Bibb lettuce

sauce
1 cup tomato catsup
1 teaspoon onion juice
½ teaspoon garlic powder
1 tablespoon lemon juice
1 teaspoon chili powder
Several drops Tabasco

Early in the day wash shrimp well; cook them in boiling salted water 4 minutes. Drain and refrigerate. Combine sauce ingredients in a small bowl; mix well. Chill.

At serving time arrange shrimp and lettuce on one large plate or on individual plates, serving sauce in a small cup or bowl in center of plate. Garnish with fresh dill, if available. Makes 4 to 6 servings.

spiced cocktail nuts
cacahuetes

4 tablespoons butter
1 tablespoon Worchestershire sauce
½ teaspoon hot pepper sauce
1 tablespoon seasoned salad salt
1 teaspoon salt
½ teaspoon garlic salt
¼ teaspoon pepper
1 pound walnuts, almonds, or filberts (a mixture of nuts is also good)

Melt butter; add remaining ingredients, except nuts. Stir until well-blended. Add nuts; toss. Cook over low heat 15 minutes, stirring occasionally. Cook 5 minutes in a 350°F oven, until crispy. Drain on paper towels.

Store in an airtight container. Makes 4½ cups.

pickled fish cocktail
seviche

1 pound very fresh fillets of flounder or other firm-fleshed white fish, such as sole or pompano
1 cup lime juice, freshly squeezed
2 medium tomatoes, peeled, seeded, and chopped
2 tablespoons chopped onion
2 canned jalapeño chilies, finely chopped
¼ cup olive oil
1 tablespoon vinegar
½ teaspoon basil
1 teaspoon oregano
¾ teaspoon salt
¼ teaspoon white pepper
½ red pepper, cut in strips
½ green pepper, cut in strips
¼ cup sliced pimiento-stuffed green olives

Wash fish well. Remove any skin or bones; cut fish into small pieces; place in small, deep, glass bowl. Pour lime juice over fish and refrigerate for 6 hours, stirring occasionally.

At least ½ hour before serving, add tomatoes, onion, chilies, olive oil, vinegar, basil, oregano, salt, and white pepper; toss gently. Refrigerate until serving time.

Serve fish cocktail in a decorative pottery or glass serving dish garnished with the red and green peppers and sliced olives. Makes 6 to 8 servings.

pickled fish cocktail

pork tidbits
carnitas

1½ pounds boneless pork (leg, shoulder, or loin)
Water
1 teaspoon salt
½ teaspoon coriander
½ teaspoon crumbled oregano
½ teaspoon crumbled dried cilantro
½ teaspoon pepper

Cut meat into thin finger strips approximately 2 inches long and ½ inch wide, with a little fat on each piece. Place meat in a large saucepan. Add enough water to cover ¾ of the meat. Add salt, coriander, oregano, and cilantro; stir well. Bring to a boil over moderate heat; cook, stirring occasionally, until all water has evaporated. Reduce heat to low; slowly brown meat in its own fat. Sprinkle with pepper while browning.

Serve tidbits hot as an appetizer with sauces for dipping, such as Hot Dip (see Index) or jalapeño sauce, or use as a filling for tacos. Makes 4 servings.

meat pies
empanadas

These meat pies are large. They can be served as a substantial first course with a light supper, or cut into pieces and served. These would make a delicious luncheon dish, so make enough for leftovers!

1 10-ounce package frozen patty shells
1 cup diced cooked roast beef
1 onion, chopped
1 clove garlic, minced
2 tablespoons butter
½ teaspoon salt
¼ teaspoon pepper
¼ teaspoon thyme
¼ teaspoon cumin
¼ teaspoon chili powder
2 dashes Tabasco
1 tomato, peeled and chopped
¼ cup raisins
¼ cup sliced stuffed green olives
2 hard-cooked eggs, diced
Milk

Remove patty shells from freezer and allow to stand at room temperature until soft enough to roll.

Meanwhile, prepare the filling. In a small skillet sauté beef, onion, and garlic in butter over low heat 5 minutes. Add salt, pepper, thyme, cumin, chili powder, Tabasco, and tomato. Reduce heat to simmer; cook for 10 minutes.

Meanwhile, soak raisins in boiling water until plump. Drain well.

Combine meat mixture, raisins, olives, and eggs; set aside.

Roll each patty shell on a floured pastry cloth to a rectangle approximately 5 × 8 inches. Place ⅓ cup filling on one half of the rectangle. Fold to form a turnover. Seal with milk.

Preheat oven to 450°F. Place turnovers on an ungreased cookie sheet; brush with milk. Place in oven; immediately reduce heat to 400°F; bake for 20 to 25 minutes or until well-browned and puffed. Makes 6 servings.

"little fat ones"
gorditas

2 cups Masa Harina
½ cup sifted all-purpose flour
½ teaspoon salt
1½ cups warm water
3 tablespoons melted lard
Oil for frying
1 pound Mexican pork
  sausage
¼ pound cheddar cheese,
  grated
1 small onion, chopped
1 4-ounce can Green Chili
  Salsa

Combine Masa Harina, flour, and salt in a mixing bowl. Add water and melted lard. Mix well; knead until well-blended. Divide into 15 equal pieces. Flatten each piece into a 3-inch circle. Bake on ungreased griddle over medium heat until very slightly browned. While still warm, pinch up edges between your thumb and fingers to form a rim all around tortillas. Punch up small mounds in centers so that rounds look like small sombreros. Set aside until serving time.

At serving time, fry sausage; drain. Keep them warm.

In a small skillet heat 2 inches oil to 375°F. Fry in deep fat until golden brown. Drain. Fill brims of sombreros with sausage; top with grated cheese and onion; drizzle with a little of the Chili Salsa. Makes 15.

meat pies

soups and dry soups

mexican meatball soup
albondigas

broth
**2 10¾-ounce cans condensed
    beef broth**
2 soup cans water
1 bay leaf
¼ cup dry sherry
½ cup tomato sauce

meatbalis
¾ pound ground beef
¾ pound lean ground pork
⅓ cup raw long-grain rice
1½ teaspoons salt
¼ teaspoon pepper
1 egg, slightly beaten
1 tablespoon chopped mint

**2 tablespoons chopped parsley
    for garnish**

Combine broth ingredients in large saucepan. Bring mixture to a boil over moderate heat.

Meanwhile, combine meatball ingredients. Mix well; form into meatballs, using approximately 1 tablespoon meat mixture for each meatball. Add meatballs, a few at a time, to hot broth. When all meatballs have been added, cover saucepan; reduce heat to low. Cook for 30 minutes. Remove bay leaf.

Garnish soup with parsley. Serve with crusty bread. Makes 4 to 6 servings.

mexican soup

sopa mexicana

1 clove garlic, peeled
¾ teaspoon salt
4 tablespoons butter
1 medium onion, chopped
1 fresh hot green pepper, chopped
½ pound baked ham, chopped
1 cup chopped unpeeled zucchini squash
4½ cups beef broth
¼ teaspoon crumbled thyme
2 sweet red peppers, cleaned, seeded, and chopped
3 tablespoons tomato paste
1 16½-ounce can whole-kernel corn
Salt and pepper
2 tablespoons chopped fresh parsley

On a cutting board sprinkle the garlic clove with ¾ teaspoon salt; mash with blade of a knife.

Melt butter in a Dutch oven; add garlic, onion, hot pepper, ham, and zucchini. Sauté over moderate heat for 10 minutes. Add beef broth and thyme; simmer for 15 minutes. Add sweet peppers, tomato paste, and corn (along with the liquid from the can); stir well. Cook for 15 minutes more. Season to taste with salt and pepper.

Garnish soup with parsley. Makes 4 to 6 servings.

Note: If fresh hot peppers are not available, substitute 1 canned green chili, chopped, for the hot pepper. Three canned pimientos (chopped) may be substituted for the red peppers if necessary, but first check the frozen-foods section of your local market. Frozen chopped red peppers are now available all year round in some places.

hominy soup

pozole

This soup is traditionally served in Mexican homes on Christmas Eve when the family returns from church.

3 pigs feet, split, or 2 large, fresh pork hocks
1 stewing chicken (about 4 pounds), cut up
1 pound lean pork (Boston butt), cut up
2 medium onions, finely chopped
2 cloves garlic, chopped
3 quarts water
1 tablespoon salt
4 red chili pods
1 29-ounce can white hominy, drained

garnish
1 cup sliced radishes
1 cup shredded lettuce
½ cup sliced green onions
½ cup shredded Jack cheese

In large kettle combine pigs feet or pork hocks, chicken, pork, onions, garlic, water, salt, and chili pods. Bring to a boil; reduce heat to low. Cook for 2 hours. Add hominy; continue cooking until meat starts to fall off bone (3 to 3½ hours total cooking time). Remove meat from broth; cool meat and broth in refrigerator several hours or overnight.

Discard chili pods; remove meat from bones. Skim fat from surface of broth. At serving time, add meat to broth; heat.

Serve soup hot in soup bowls with hot tortillas. Pass the garnishes in separate bowls, so that each diner can garnish his plate to his own taste. Makes 8 to 10 servings.

corn soup
sopa de elote

4 cups fresh corn, cut from the cob
1 cup chicken stock
¼ cup butter
½ cup chopped green onions
3½ cups milk
½ teaspoon salt
3 tablespoons chopped green chilies
6 tablespoons sour cream
Tostadas
Chopped parsley

Combine corn and chicken stock in blender; blend to a smooth puree.

Melt butter in large saucepan. Wilt green onions in butter. Add corn puree; simmer for 5 minutes or until thickened. Add milk and salt; cook 15 minutes over low heat.

Divide chilies among 6 soup bowls. Pour soup into bowls. Garnish each with a tablespoon of sour cream, a few tostadas, and a little chopped parsley. Serve. Makes 6 servings.

lentil soup
sopa de lentejas

1 cup lentils
1 quart water
5 slices bacon, cut into squares
1 medium onion, chopped
½ cup sliced carrots
½ cup sliced celery
1 8-ounce can tomato sauce
3 medium tomatoes, chopped
1 teaspoon salt
1 bay leaf
1 beef bouillon cube

Soak lentils in water 30 minutes.

Sauté bacon and onion until bacon is crisp and onions are transparent. Add water, lentils, carrots, celery, tomato sauce, chopped tomatoes, salt, bay leaf, and bouillon cube. Simmer about 1½ hours. Makes 8 1-cup servings.

cold tomato and vegetable soup
gazpacho

8 large tomatoes, peeled and seeded
2 medium cucumbers, peeled and seeded
2 large green peppers, seeds and pith removed
1 cup finely chopped sweet onion
3 cloves garlic, peeled
⅓ cup olive oil
1 cup rich beef bouillon
½ tablespoon lemon juice
Salt and freshly ground black pepper

Chop about ⅔ of the tomatoes fine. Set aside in large bowl.

Finely chop cucumbers, peppers, and onion, adding each vegetable with its juices to the large bowl.

Puree remaining tomatoes, garlic, and olive oil; pour over chopped vegetables along with bouillon and lemon juice. Add salt and pepper to taste. Refrigerate for several hours.

Before serving, sample and adjust seasonings; add a little bouillon to thin the soup, if needed. Makes 6 servings.

chicken soup with vermicelli
caldo de pollo con fideos

6 cups chicken stock
1 whole chicken breast, split (about 1 pound)
¼ pound vermicelli
¼ cup vegetable oil
1 large tomato, peeled, seeded, and chopped
1 ripe avocado
2 hot green chilies, chopped
Salt and pepper to taste

Early in the day heat stock to boiling in large saucepan. Add chicken, reduce heat to low, and simmer for 25 minutes. Remove and cool chicken. Skin, remove from bones, and shred the meat.

At dinner time break vermicelli into 2-inch lengths.

Heat oil in small skillet; lightly brown vermicelli. Drain on paper towels.

Meanwhile, again heat stock to boiling. Add vermicelli; cook until tender. Add tomato and chicken shreds; heat through.

Peel and seed avocado; cut into chunks. Add avocado, chilies, salt, and pepper. Heat through.

Serve soup hot with tostadas. Makes 6 servings.

avocado cream
crema de aguacates

1½ tablespoons butter or margarine
1½ tablespoons flour
2½ cups hot chicken stock
1 very ripe avocado (large)
2 tablespoons lime juice
¾ cup heavy cream
¼ cup sherry
½ teaspoon salt
Dash white pepper

Melt butter or margarine in large saucepan. Add flour; cook until bubbly. Add hot chicken stock slowly, stirring constantly, and cook over low heat until slightly thickened.

Peel avocado, remove 4 thin slices for garnish, and dip in lime juice.

Mash remaining avocado and add remaining lime juice to keep it from turning brown. Add avocado pulp, cream, sherry, salt, and pepper.

Serve cream hot, garnished with an avocado slice. Makes 4 servings.

mexican rice I
arroz mexicano I

In Mexico, this would be called a *sopa seca* (dry soup) and served as a separate course. However, it also makes a delicious accompaniment for meat or fowl.

3 tablespoons vegetable oil
½ cup chopped onion
1 clove garlic, minced
1 cup raw long-grain rice
¼ cup chopped red pepper
½ teaspoon salt
Dash cayenne pepper
2 cups boiling water
2 teaspoons chicken-broth granules
¾ cup frozen peas and carrots, thawed
1 small tomato, peeled, seeded, and chopped (about ⅓ cup)

Heat oil in heavy frying pan over medium heat. Add onion, garlic, rice, and red pepper; sauté until onion is limp and rice is opaque. Add salt, cayenne pepper, boiling water, and chicken-broth granules. Cover; cook 20 minutes or until liquid is absorbed. Add peas and carrots and tomato. Cook, stirring, just until vegetables are heated through.

Serve rice immediately. Makes 4 to 6 servings.

Picture on opposite page: mexican rice 1

mexican rice II
arroz mexicano II

3 tablespoons olive oil
1 cup raw long-grain rice
¼ cup chopped green onions
¼ teaspoon garlic powder
2 cups chicken broth

3 tablespoons tomato paste
½ teaspoon ground cumin
¼ cup grated Jack cheese
Chopped green onions for
  garnish

Heat oil in 2-quart saucepan over moderate heat. Add rice; sauté until very lightly browned. Add onions, garlic powder, and chicken broth; stir well. Stir in tomato paste and cumin. Bring mixture to a boil. Cover; reduce heat to low. Cook for 20 minutes or until all liquid is absorbed.

Place rice mixture in small ovenproof (preferably earthenware) casserole. Top with grated cheese. Bake in 350°F oven until cheese melts.

Garnish rice with green onions; serve. Makes 4 servings.

cumin rice
arroz de comino

3 tablespoons olive oil
1 green pepper, chopped
1 red pepper, chopped
½ cup chopped onion
1 clove garlic, chopped
1 cup raw long-grain rice
¾ teaspoon ground cumin
2 teaspoons chicken-broth
  granules
2 cups boiling water

Heat oil in ovenproof casserole. Add pepper, onion, garlic, and rice until rice is lightly browned and onion is limp. Add cumin, chicken-broth granules, and boiling water. Cover tightly; bake at 350°F for 30 minutes or until all liquid is absorbed.

Serve rice as a side dish with meat, fish, or fowl. Makes 4 servings.

dry soup with vermicelli
sopa seca con fideos

½ pound chorizo (Mexican
  pork sausage)
6 tablespoons olive oil
½ pound vermicelli
1 small onion, chopped
1 cup canned tomatoes
2 cups chicken broth
Salt and pepper to taste
Parmesan cheese
Chopped parsley

Brown the chorizo; drain and set it aside.

Heat oil in heavy skillet. Sauté vermicelli over medium heat until golden. Drain; place in 2-quart casserole.

Pour off all except 1 tablespoon oil. Sauté onion until limp. Add tomatoes, chicken broth, and salt and pepper to taste. Bring to a boil. Pour over vermicelli. Add chorizo; stir well. Cover and bake at 350°F for 15 minutes or until all liquid is absorbed.

Sprinkle soup with Parmesan cheese and chopped parsley; serve. Makes 6 servings.

spanish stew
cocido

This hearty vegetable and beef soup-stew is of Spanish origin, with a few Mexican additions!

2 pounds beef shanks
3 quarts water
2 cloves garlic, peeled and chopped
1 onion, sliced
1 tablespoon salt
8 peppercorns
6 tablespoons tomato puree
3 medium carrots, peeled and sliced
3 zucchini, sliced
3 cups fresh green beans, nipped and cut into 1-inch lengths
2 medium potatoes, peeled and sliced
3 ears of corn, cut into 1-inch pieces

Brown the beef shanks in a roasting pan in a 450°F oven.

In a large soup pot combine browned beef, pan drippings, water, garlic, onion, salt, and peppercorns. Bring to a boil, reduce heat to low, cover, and cook 2½ hours or until meat is very tender. Remove meat. Strain broth and return it to kettle. Add tomato puree; bring to a boil. Add vegetables. Reduce heat to low; cook, covered, 30 to 45 minutes or until vegetables are tender.

Cut meat from bones; add to soup. Heat through.

Serve stew with your favorite chili sauce. Makes 6 to 8 servings.

salads

molded avocado ring
ensalada aguacate

1½ cups mashed avocado
   (about 2 avocados)
2 tablespoons lemon juice
1 package lemon gelatin
¾ cup boiling water
1 cup sour cream
¾ cup mayonnaise
1 tablespoon onion juice
Dash cayenne pepper
2 tablespoons finely chopped
   green pepper
Mayonnaise
Paprika

Peel and seed avocados, sprinkle with lemon juice, and mash well. Force them through a sieve, or puree in an electric blender.

Dissolve gelatin in boiling water. Add avocado, sour cream, mayonnaise, onion juice, cayenne pepper, and green pepper.

Lightly oil ring mold; pour in mixture. Chill it overnight. Unmold onto a large plate.

Garnish with whole black olives, cherry tomatoes, and Bibb lettuce.

Place a small bowl in the center of the ring; fill it with mayonnaise dusted with paprika. Makes 6 servings.

chili with salad
chile con ensalada

1 small head lettuce, in chunks
3 cups corn chips
1 large tomato, chopped
1 avocado, sliced
4 ounces chorizo, cooked and crumbled
¼ cup sliced ripe olives
½ cup shredded cheddar cheese
1 16-ounce can chili con carne with beans

Place lettuce chunks in bowl. Decorate with all other ingredients except chili.

Heat chili and pour over all other ingredients. Serve at once. Makes 6 servings.

cumin salad
ensalada comino

2 medium tomatoes, diced
½ cup chopped onion
½ cup sliced ripe olives
¼ cup chopped fresh parsley
2 cups sliced iceberg lettuce

salad dressing
¼ cup olive oil
2 tablespoons lemon juice
Salt and pepper to taste
½ teaspoon ground cumin
1 teaspoon crumbled dried sage leaves
⅛ teaspoon garlic salt

Layer tomatoes, onion, olives, parsley, and lettuce in salad bowl.

Combine olive oil, lemon juice, salt and pepper, cumin, sage, and garlic salt, mixing well. Pour over salad. Refrigerate 1 hour before serving. Makes 4 servings.

orange and onion salad
ensalada de naranjas y cebollas

This salad can be prepared several hours ahead of the meal.

4 large oranges
1 Bermuda onion, sliced
1 medium cucumber, sliced
1 small green pepper, peeled, seeded, and chopped

salad dressing
⅓ cup vegetable oil
¼ cup wine vinegar
1 teaspoon sugar
½ teaspoon salt
¼ teaspoon chili powder

Peel oranges, removing as much white membrane as possible. Slice; remove seeds. Arrange oranges, onion, and cucumber in alternating layers in a serving dish. Sprinkle with green pepper. Pour dressing over all; garnish with endive. Refrigerate until serving time. Makes 6 servings.

garbanzo salad
ensalada de garbanzo

A hearty salad!

1 15-ounce can garbanzo beans, drained
⅛ teaspoon garlic powder
½ teaspoon chili powder
2 tablespoons oil
2 tablespoons wine vinegar
1 tablespoon dried parsley
¾ cup chopped celery
1 4-ounce can pimientos, drained and chopped
3 green onions, chopped
Salt and pepper to taste

Rinse garbanzos in cold water; drain. Combine beans with other ingredients; allow to stand several hours. Stir periodically to be sure all flavors are well-mixed. Serve in lettuce cups. Makes 4 servings.

exotic
fruit salad
ensalada de frutas exotico

salad
1 head Bibb lettuce
½ cup sliced radishes
**½ medium cucumber, thinly
 sliced**
2 small tomatoes, sliced
**1 green pepper, cleaned,
 seeded, and cut into slivers**
1 cup diced fresh pineapple
**1 cup fresh strawberries, cut
 in half**
**½ cup drained mandarin
 oranges**
½ ripe avocado
1 large peach
2 tablespoons lemon juice

salad dressing
½ cup finely minced onion
½ teaspoon prepared mustard
6 tablespoons lemon juice
Salt
White pepper
3 tablespoons vegetable oil

¼ cup chopped parsley
**2 tablespoons chopped fresh
 dill**
**½ teaspoon crumbled dried
 tarragon**

First prepare dressing. Combine onion, mustard, lemon juice, salt and white pepper to taste, oil, parsley, dill, and tarragon. Mix well. Let stand at least ½ hour to blend flavors.

Wash lettuce, dry, break into bite-size pieces, and place in large salad bowl. Add radishes, cucumber, tomatoes, green pepper, pineapple, strawberries, and mandarin oranges.

Just before serving, peel avocado half and peach, cut in wedges, and dip in lemon juice. Add to salad.

Mix dressing again; pour over salad. Toss and serve. Makes 6 servings.

melon
salad
ensalada de tlacopan

1 tablespoon horseradish
**⅛ teaspoon finely crushed red
 chilies**
½ teaspoon salt
1 teaspoon sugar
½ cup olive oil
**¼ cup mild fruit vinegar
 (preferably pineapple or
 pear)**
½ ripe medium cantaloupe
½ medium head lettuce

In jar of electric blender combine horseradish, chilies, salt, sugar, oil, and vinegar; blend. Let stand 20 minutes.

Peel cantaloupe; slice into thin wedges.

Shred lettuce and arrange on serving plates. Top with cantaloupe wedges.

Blend dressing again; pour it over salads. Makes 4 servings.

potato salad
ensalada de papas

4 medium potatoes
1 small onion, chopped
½ cup sliced ripe olives
½ cup chopped parsley
¼ cup olive oil
3 tablespoons red wine
   vinegar
½ teaspoon chili powder
½ teaspoon salt
¼ teaspoon pepper
2 hard-cooked eggs, chopped

Scrub potatoes and cook unpeeled in boiling, salted water 30 to 40 minutes or until tender. Cool, peel, and dice.

Gently combine potatoes, onion, olives, and parsley.

Mix together olive oil, vinegar, chili powder, salt, and pepper. Add dressing and eggs to salad; toss gently. Chill.

Serve salad on lettuce leaves, garnished with tomatoes. Makes 4 servings.

maximilian's salad
ensalada maximiliano

Mexican cooks took the best from the French and Italian cooks of Maximilian's court and incorporated them into their own cuisine.

1 large head lettuce (or 8 cups
   mixed salad greens)
1 medium Bermuda onion,
   sliced
1 clove garlic, peeled
1 teaspoon salt

1 tablespoon sugar
½ teaspoon paprika
½ cup olive oil
¼ cup lemon juice
1 3-ounce package Roquefort
   cheese, crumbled

Clean lettuce, removing any brown or damaged leaves. Wash well; drain. Shake dry; tear into bite-size pieces.

Combine lettuce and sliced onion in large salad bowl. Sprinkle garlic clove with salt; mash with blade of a knife.

In blender jar combine mashed garlic, salt, sugar, paprika, olive oil, and lemon juice; whirl until blended. Pour over salad; toss.

Sprinkle salad with Roquefort cheese. Serve with toasted tortillas. Makes 6 servings.

pickled corn salad
ensalada de maíz en escabeche

½ cup chopped onions
½ cup diced green peppers
4 tablespoons chopped
   pimiento
3 tablespoons sugar
¾ teaspoon salt

½ teaspoon celery salt
½ teaspoon dry mustard
½ cup cider vinegar
½ cup water
3 cups frozen whole-kernel
   corn

Combine all ingredients except frozen corn; bring to a boil. Lower heat, cover pan, and simmer for 12 minutes, stirring occasionally. Add frozen corn; raise heat. When boiling resumes, lower heat; simmer until corn is just tender (2 or 3 minutes). Drain.

Serve salad hot, or refrigerate and serve on lettuce leaves. Makes 4 to 6 servings.

peppers filled with shrimp salad
chiles rellenos con ensalada camerónes

4 large green peppers
2 cups cooked medium shrimp
1 tablespoon lemon juice
2 tablespoons chopped green pepper
2 tablespoons chopped red pepper (or substitute pimiento)
½ cup chopped celery
¼ cup finely chopped onion
1 tablespoon chopped fresh cilantro
½ teaspoon salt
¼ teaspoon pepper
¼ cup mayonnaise
¼ cup sour cream
4 thin lemon slices

At least 2 hours prior to serving, prepare and chill salad. First place peppers upright on cutting board. Slice down through stem, cutting away ⅓ of pepper. Reserve the piece of pepper to chop for the salad or for later use. Remove seeds and membrane from inside peppers. Blanch peppers in 1 inch boiling water 4 minutes. Immediately plunge them into ice water; drain well.

Meanwhile, toss together shrimp, lemon juice, green pepper, red pepper, celery, onion, cilantro, salt, and pepper.

Mix together mayonnaise and sour cream. Add to shrimp mixture; blend well. Chill shrimp salad and peppers until serving time.

To serve, stuff pepper shells with shrimp mixture; garnish with a lemon slice. Makes 4 servings.

salad monterey-style
ensalada monterey

1 pound zucchini squash
1 avocado
2 tablespoons chopped onion
2 whole roasted peeled California chilies, seeded and chopped
¼ cup salad oil
2 tablespoons vinegar
1 teaspoon salt
⅛ teaspoon pepper
¼ teaspoon chili powder
¼ teaspoon sugar
1 3-ounce package cream cheese
Lettuce
1 tomato, cut in wedges
Pimiento-stuffed olives

Clean zucchini; slice into ½-inch-thick slices. Cook in boiling salted water until just tender. Drain.

Peel and cube avocado; combine with zucchini, onion, and chilies.

Combine salad oil, vinegar, salt, pepper, chili powder, and sugar; pour over vegetables. Mix gently. Refrigerate for 20 to 25 minutes.

Cut cream cheese into ½-inch cubes.

Place lettuce in serving bowl.

Combine salad mixture with tomato wedges and cream cheese. Place in serving bowl; garnish salad with sliced olives. Makes 6 servings.

marinated
beef salad
*carne ensalada a la
vinagreta*

This salad is a cool and imaginative way to use leftover roast beef.

salad
3 cups cubed cooked lean beef
½ cup chopped onion
2 tablespoons chopped parsley
**1 sweet red pepper, seeded
  and chopped**
1 medium tomato, chopped

salad dressing
½ cup olive oil
¼ cup wine vinegar
½ teaspoon salt
¼ teaspoon pepper
½ teaspoon crumbled oregano
½ teaspoon prepared mustard

garnish
1 head Boston lettuce
1 large tomato, cut in wedges

Combine beef, onion, parsley, red pepper, and tomato, tossing well.

Combine olive oil, vinegar, salt, pepper, oregano, and mustard; pour over salad, tossing well. Refrigerate at least 3 hours.

At serving time line serving dish with lettuce leaves, fill with salad, and garnish with tomato wedges. Serve with plenty of crusty bread. Makes 4 servings.

mixed green
salad
ensalada verde mixta

**1 head Bibb lettuce (or ½
  head iceberg lettuce)**
**2 green peppers, cleaned,
  seeded, and cut into strips**
4 small tomatoes, sliced
**2 small onions, sliced and
  separated into rings**
2 hard-cooked eggs, sliced
**½ cup sliced stuffed green
  olives**
**½ medium cucumber, peeled,
  seeded, and cut into chunks**

salad dressing

4 tablespoons olive oil
**3 tablespoons tarragon
  vinegar**
½ teaspoon salt
**¼ teaspoon fresh ground
  pepper**

1 clove garlic, crushed
¼ teaspoon crushed oregano
**1 tablespoon chopped fresh
  parsley**

Wash lettuce; clean, dry, and tear into bite-size pieces. Place in salad bowl, add peppers, tomatoes, onions, eggs, olives, and cucumber. Refrigerate.

Combine all dressing ingredients; mix well.

At serving time toss salad at the table with prepared dressing. Makes 4 servings.

marinated beef salad

mixed green salad

28

meat dishes

marinated beef roast
carne de vaca asada

1 clove garlic, minced	2 tablespoons lemon juice
1 teaspoon ground black pepper	1 4-pound rolled rump roast
1 bay leaf	3 tablespoons olive oil
1½ cups dry red wine	2 tablespoons flour
	2 tablespoons water

Combine garlic, pepper, bay leaf, wine, and lemon juice in an enamelware pan or deep glass casserole. Add roast; turn it several times to coat with mixture. Cover; allow to marinate in refrigerator at least 24 hours, turning occasionally.

Heat oil over moderate heat.

Remove roast from marinade and pat dry. Brown on all sides in hot oil.

Meanwhile, preheat oven to 375°F.

Pour marinade over roast in Dutch oven; cover tightly. Place in oven; cook for 2 hours. Uncover; bake for 30 minutes more. Transfer pan to stove; remove meat to warm platter.

Make a paste with flour and water; thicken the pan gravy.

Slice the roast and serve with the gravy and oven-fried potato wedges. Makes 8 to 10 servings.

swiss steak mexican-style
biftec suizio mexicano

3 tablespoons flour
½ teaspoon seasoned salt
⅛ teaspoon pepper
1½ pounds bottom round
    steak
3 tablespoons oil
1 large onion, sliced
1 clove garlic, minced
1½ cups sliced fresh
    mushrooms
2 cups canned tomatoes
1½ teaspoons chili powder
1 teaspoon sugar
¼ cup red wine
1 tablespoon water
Salt and pepper to taste

Combine 2 tablespoons of the flour, the seasoned salt, and pepper. Dredge steak in flour mixture.

Heat oil in electric skillet or large, heavy skillet. Brown steaks well on both sides. Remove from pan. Add onion, garlic, and mushrooms; sauté for 5 minutes, stirring occasionally.

Puree tomatoes in electric blender with chili powder, sugar, and wine. Add to vegetables in skillet.

Return meat to skillet. Coat with sauce. Bring to a boil, reduce heat to low, and cover. Simmer for 2 to 2½ hours or until tender. Combine flour and water to form a paste. Remove steaks from skillet; keep them warm. Slowly add flour and water paste to gravy, stirring well. Cook over low heat until thickened.

Serve the steaks and gravy with hot cooked rice. Makes 4 servings.

ranch-style steaks
biftecs rancheros

sauce
2 tablespoons olive oil
1 green pepper, cleaned,
    seeded, and chopped
1 clove garlic, minced
½ cup chopped onion
2 hot peppers, stemmed,
    seeded, and chopped
¼ cup tomato catsup
1 cup beef broth
Salt and pepper to taste
½ teaspoon paprika

steaks
4 fillet steaks (3 ounces each)
4 tablespoons cooking oil
Salt and pepper to taste
Parsley, pickled hot peppers,
    and tomato wedges

Heat olive oil in small skillet. Add vegetables; sauté for 3 minutes. Add catsup, broth, salt and pepper to taste, and paprika. Reduce heat to low; simmer mixture while cooking steaks.

Slightly flatten steaks. Wipe with a damp cloth; pat dry with a paper towel.

Heat cooking oil in heavy skillet over moderately high heat. Sauté steaks for 3 minutes on each side; transfer to a warm platter.

Top steaks with the sauce. Garnish with parsley, tomato wedges, and hot peppers. Makes 4 servings.

stuffed flank steak with american sauce

aldilla rellenos con salsa americana

1 2½-pound flank steak
1 teaspoon salt
¼ teaspoon freshly ground pepper

½ teaspoon thyme
1 clove garlic, minced
¼ cup wine vinegar

stuffing

2 tablespoons butter
1 medium onion, chopped
½ cup chopped walnuts

⅓ cup chopped parsley
1 egg, beaten
1½ cups bread crumbs

3 tablespoons olive oil
2 cups beef broth

1 cup water
1 bay leaf

The day before serving wipe flank steak with a damp cloth and pound with a mallet or the edge of a cleaver to an even thickness. Combine salt, pepper, thyme, garlic, and vinegar. Put steak in a glass or ceramic dish; pour marinade over meat. Cover and refrigerate.

Bring steak to room temperature while making the stuffing.

Melt butter in heavy skillet. Sauté onion until limp. Combine walnuts, parsley, egg, and bread crumbs in mixing bowl. Add onion and butter; mix well.

Pat steak dry with paper towels; place on flat surface. Spoon stuffing down center of steak; roll steak to completely enclose stuffing. Secure with string tied 1-inch apart the length of the steak. Secure ends of steak with skewers.

Heat olive oil in skillet; brown the steak on all sides, and place in casserole. Pour beef broth and water over steak; add bay leaf to liquid. Cover; bake at 375°F for 1¼ hours or until tender. Remove from pan, cut strings, and let stand 10 minutes before slicing.

Serve garnished with sautéed peppers and American Sauce. Makes 6 servings.

american sauce

1 tablespoon butter or margarine
1 tablespoon flour
½ teaspoon salt

⅛ teaspoon pepper
1 cup tomato sauce
½ cup heavy cream

Melt butter in small saucepan. Add flour, salt, and pepper; stir well. Cook until bubbly. Add tomato sauce; cook, stirring constantly, over low heat until thickened. Remove from heat. Quickly stir in cream. Serve.

chili
con carne
chile con carne

1½ pounds stew meat, cubed
2 tablespoons oil
1 medium onion, chopped
1 8-ounce can tomato sauce
1 6-ounce can tomato paste
1 1-pound can kidney beans
1 tablespoon chili powder
½ teaspoon hot-pepper sauce
¾ cup water (more as needed)

Brown stew meat in oil. Add onion; cook until tender. Add tomato sauce, tomato paste, kidney beans, chili powder, and hot-pepper sauce. Mix in ¾ cup water. Cover; simmer for 2½ hours or more, until meat is tender. Add more water as needed. Makes 6 to 8 servings.

stuffed
chilies
chiles rellenos

These may be prepared ahead and warmed in the oven or a chafing dish.

2 medium onions, chopped
1 clove garlic, crushed
2 tablespoons oil
½ pound ground beef
½ pound ground pork
1 cup chopped fresh tomatoes
1 teaspoon salt

½ teaspoon pepper
4 tablespoons sliced almonds
4 tablespoons raisins
8 whole canned chilies
4 eggs
½ cup flour
Oil for frying

Sauté onions and garlic in 2 tablespoons oil until onion is transparent. Add ground meats; stir until meat is crumbly. Add chopped tomatoes, seasonings, almonds, and raisins. Simmer.

Remove chili seeds, leaving chili skins whole. Stuff chilies with meat filling; roll them well in flour. Then dip them in the following egg batter: Beat egg whites until stiff; beat egg yolks; combine egg yolks with egg whites.

Fry chilies in deep fat at 375°F until golden brown. Remove; drain on toweling. Makes 8 servings.

meat loaf
mexican-style
albóndigon mexicana

1½ pounds meat-loaf mix (a mixture of ground beef, veal, and pork) or ground beef
1 cup soft bread crumbs
1 small onion, chopped
1 10-ounce can tomatoes and green chilies

1 egg, lightly beaten
¼ teaspoon garlic powder
½ teaspoon salt
¼ teaspoon pepper
2 hard-cooked eggs, cut in half lengthwise
¼ cup sliced pimiento-stuffed green olives

Combine meat, bread crumbs, onion, ½ can of tomatoes and green chilies, egg, garlic powder, salt, and pepper; mix well.

Pack half of mixture into an 8 × 4 × 2-inch loaf pan. Arrange hard-cooked eggs in a single row down center of loaf. Arrange olives in rows on either side of eggs. Press eggs and olives lightly into meat mixture. Top with remaining meat mixture. Pour remaining half can of tomatoes and green chilies over meat loaf. Bake at 350°F for 1 hour. Makes 4 to 5 servings.

tamales

Tamales are of Aztec origin and provide an easy and filling dish to use up small quantities of leftover meat and poultry.

24 corn husks (dried) or 24 6-inch squares of cooking parchment

tamale dough
1 cup lard
2½ cups instant Masa Harina
½ teaspoon salt
1¾ cups chicken broth

tamale filling
1½ cups Pork in Red Chili Sauce (see Index) or Mexican Meat Hash (see Index) or any Mexican meat and sauce dish or 1½ cups
cooked shredded meat mixed with Red Chili Sauce to moisten or 24 small cheese slices (1 × 3 inches)
24 small strips of green chili

Soak corn husks in hot water to cover, if used.

Next make the dough. Beat lard with electric mixer until light. Add masa, salt, and chicken broth; beat until light and fluffy. Divide into 24 equal parts.

Drain corn husks; pat dry. Place each portion masa dough on parchment square or corn husk; spread to form a 4-inch square, keeping one side even with one edge of the paper or husk. Top with 1 tablespoon of filling or 1 slice of cheese plus one strip of chili pepper. Roll up as for a jelly roll, starting with the side of the dough that is even with the side of the paper or husk. Fold the ends over, sealing well.

The tamales are cooked by steaming. A steamer pot is ideal (the kind used for crabs or corn), but one can be easily improvised. Select a large, deep pot. Place a vegetable steaming basket or metal colander in bottom of pan. Line steamer or colander with any leftover corn husks. Bring 1 to 2 inches of water to boil in bottom of kettle or steamer pot.

Meanwhile, place tamales upright in steamer, packing tightly. Place basket in steamer kettle; cover tightly. Steam for 1 hour or until dough no longer sticks to paper.

Serve tamales hot with chili sauce (for example: Red Chili Sauce). Makes 24 tamales.

red chili sauce
salsa chile rojo

5 dried Ancho chilies
1 cup boiling water
1 teaspoon crushed red chili peppers
1 cup cut-up drained canned Italian plum tomatoes
½ cup chopped onion
1 clove garlic, minced
¼ cup olive oil
1 teaspoon sugar
½ teaspoon salt
⅛ teaspoon pepper
1 tablespoon red wine vinegar

Under cold running water, remove the stems from the Ancho chilies. Tear each in half; remove seeds and thick veins. Tear into pieces; place into small mixing bowl. Pour boiling water over chilies; let stand 30 minutes. Drain chilies, reserving ¼ cup liquid.

Combine chilies, reserved liquid, crushed chili, tomatoes, onion, and garlic in blender jar. Puree until smooth.

Heat oil in small skillet. Add puree; cook uncovered 5 minutes. Add sugar, salt, and pepper. Remove from heat; add vinegar.

Serve sauce warm. Makes 2 cups.

tamale pie
pastel tamale

½ pound ground beef
½ pound bulk pork sausage
1 large onion, sliced
⅛ teaspoon minced garlic
1 16-ounce can tomatoes with juice

1 12-ounce can whole-kernel corn, drained
1 tablespoon chili powder
1 teaspoon salt
¼ teaspoon pepper

cornmeal pastry
1 cup cornmeal
2 medium eggs

1 cup milk
18 green olives, chopped

Olive slices for garnish

Cook meats with onion and garlic until browned. Stir in tomatoes with juice, corn, and seasonings. Simmer for 10 minutes. Pour into greased oblong baking dish.

Prepare cornmeal crust by mixing cornmeal, eggs, milk, and chopped olives. Spread over hot mixture. Decorate top with a few olive slices. Bake at 350°F for 30 to 35 minutes.

Serve tamale pie warm. Makes 4 to 6 servings.

mexican meat hash
picadillo

3 tablespoons oil
½ pound lean ground pork
½ pound ground beef
1 small onion, chopped
1 clove garlic, minced
½ cup tomato catsup
1 teaspoon red wine vinegar
1 teaspoon ground cinnamon
½ teaspoon chili powder

⅛ teaspoon cumin
Pinch of ground cloves
½ cup raisins
½ teaspoon salt
¼ teaspoon ground black pepper
½ cup toasted, slivered, blanched almonds

Heat oil in large frying pan. Add meats; cook over moderate heat, stirring occasionally, until meat loses its pink color. Add onion and garlic; cook until browned. Add catsup, vinegar, cinnamon, chili powder, cumin, cloves, raisins, salt, and pepper. Stir to blend. Bring mixture to a boil. Reduce heat to simmer; cook for 15 to 20 minutes. Add almonds; stir.

Use this mixture to fill tamales, or serve with rice. Makes 4 servings.

sandwiches

This mixture also makes delicious sandwiches if served this way:

8 flour tortillas (large ones—about 8 inches in diameter)
1 recipe Mexican Meat Hash

1½ cups shredded cheddar cheese
2 cups shredded lettuce

Warm the flour tortillas in large cast-iron skillet over moderate heat about 30 seconds on each side (just heat them through and make them pliable—do not make them hard and crisp). Fill each with about ½ cup Mexican Meat Hash; top each with 3 tablespoons cheese and ¼ cup lettuce. Fold up tortillas like packages by folding bottoms and top edges in 1 inch; then pull the 2 sides to the center, overlapping each other.

beef stew mexican-style

beef stew mexican-style
estofada mexicana

This stew is moderately hot; if you prefer milder food, cut the amount of green chili salsa in half.

1½ pounds lean stewing beef,
   cut into cubes
1 large onion, sliced
1 clove garlic, minced
4 tablespoons olive oil
3 tablespoons wine vinegar
½ cup tomato sauce

1 cup red wine
1 bay leaf
1 teaspoon oregano
½ teaspoon salt
¼ teaspoon pepper
1 7-ounce can green chili salsa

Combine all ingredients in large saucepan. Bring mixture to a boil, stirring occasionally. Reduce heat to simmer; cook for 3 hours or until meat falls apart. Serve with Beer Rice. Makes 4 servings.

beer rice
2 tablespoons olive oil
1 cup raw long-grain rice
1 10¾-ounce can condensed
   onion soup
1 10¾-ounce soup can of beer

Heat olive oil in medium saucepan over moderate heat. Add rice; brown lightly, stirring constantly. Add onion soup and beer. Cover tightly; simmer for 20 to 25 minutes or until all liquid is absorbed. Makes 4 servings.

35

beef tacos
with mexican
sauce
tacos con salsa mexicana

mexican sauce
**2 cups chopped peeled
  tomatoes or 1 16-ounce can
  whole tomatoes and juice**
1 small onion, chopped
1 clove garlic, chopped
1 tablespoon chili powder
½ teaspoon oregano
1 teaspoon salt
Few drops of hot sauce

Combine all ingredients in a blender container; blend until smooth. Pour into small saucepan; simmer for 30 minutes. Use on top of taco filling. Makes 2½ to 3 cups.

taco shells
**12 to 18 fresh or frozen
  (thawed) tortillas**

To make folded, crisp-fried tacos, fry 1 corn or flour tortilla at a time in about ½ inch hot oil over medium heat, until it becomes soft (just a few seconds).

With tongs or two forks fold it in half and hold slightly, so there is a space between halves for the filling to be added later.

Fry each tortilla until crisp and light brown, turning it in oil to cook all sides. The entire cooking procedure takes only minutes for each shell. To keep fried shells warm until ready to fill, place them on a paper-towel-lined baking sheet in a 200°F oven as long as 10 or 15 minutes.

taco filling
2 pounds lean ground beef
**2 medium onions, finely
  chopped**
**1 or 2 tablespoons chili
  powder**
1 teaspoon oregano
1 teaspoon paprika
2 teaspoons salt
**1 tablespoon Worcestershire
  sauce**
⅓ cup Mexican Sauce

Brown meat and onions; drain well. Add chili powder, oregano, paprika, salt, Worcestershire sauce, and Mexican Sauce. Serve hot. Season more to taste. This freezes well. Fills 1 to 1½ dozen taco shells.

To assemble tacos, place desired amount of meat filling in center of each fried taco shell; top filling with garnishes such as shredded lettuce, shredded cheese, and Mexican Sauce. Serve tacos hot.

taco garnishes
Shredded lettuce
Shredded cheese
Chopped tomatoes
Chopped onions
Mexican Sauce

hamburger steaks mexicano

2 onions, thinly sliced (2 cups)
¼ cup butter or margarine
1 pound lean ground beef
2 tablespoons canned chopped
    green chilies
¾ teaspoon salt
½ teaspoon garlic powder
¼ teaspoon pepper

Sauté onions in butter or margarine in large skillet until lightly browned. Remove onions from pan with slotted spoon; keep them warm.

In a mixing bowl lightly combine ground beef, green chilies, salt, garlic powder, and pepper with a fork. Form into 4 thick patties.

Sauté hamburgers to desired degree of doneness over medium heat in remaining butter or margarine in skillet.

Top hamburgers with the browned onions. Serve. Makes 4 servings.

meatballs in almond sauce
albóndigas en salsa de almendra

1 egg, beaten
½ cup water
3 slices dry bread, cubed
½ teaspoon salt
⅛ teaspoon black pepper
½ teaspoon dried oregano
½ teaspoon chili powder
½ cup raisins
¾ pound ground beef
¾ pound ground pork

almond sauce
½ cup slivered almonds
1 slice dry bread, cubed
1 clove garlic, minced
2 tablespoons chopped onions
3 tablespoons meat drippings
1½ cups chicken broth
¼ cup tomato sauce
Salt and pepper to taste

For the meatballs: Mix egg, water, bread cubes, salt, pepper, oregano, chili powder, and raisins. Mix into beef and pork mixture. Shape into about 36 meatballs. Brown the meatballs. Drain, saving 3 tablespoons fat.

For the Almond Sauce: Cook almonds, bread cubes, garlic, and onions in meat drippings until browned. Remove from fat, cool, and blend to consistency of a paste by diluting with broth. Add this paste to tomato sauce, remaining broth, salt, and pepper. Simmer for 5 to 10 minutes. Makes 2 cups.

Combine Almond Sauce and meatballs. Simmer for 10 more minutes.

Serve meatballs hot. Meatballs and sauce may be served over rice. Makes 6 to 8 servings.

american enchiladas

mexican
liver
hígado a la mexicana

4 slices bacon
2 tablespoons bacon fat
1 medium onion, minced
1 pound liver, thinly sliced
1 tablespoon flour
1 tablespoon chili powder
1 teaspoon salt
1 pound canned tomatoes
   (plus liquid)
1 12-ounce can whole-kernel
   corn (drained)

Fry bacon slices, drain, and break into pieces. Save 2 tablespoons bacon fat. Sauté onion in bacon fat until tender.

Coat liver with mixture of flour, chili powder, and salt. Brown liver with onion. Add bacon, tomatoes, and corn. Simmer for 5 minutes or until tender. Makes 4 servings.

american enchiladas
enchiladas americana

For those who don't like it hot!!

cornmeal crepes	sauce
¾ cup flour	2 tablespoons olive oil
½ cup cornmeal	1 pound ground beef
1¼ cups buttermilk	¼ cup chopped onion
¼ teaspoon baking soda	1 teaspoon chili powder
3 eggs	½ teaspoon ground cumin
1 tablespoon butter, melted	½ teaspoon salt
	¼ teaspoon pepper
	1 8-ounce can tomato sauce

**Tomato wedges and parsley
for garnish**

Measure flour, cornmeal, buttermilk, baking soda, eggs, and butter into jar of electric blender. Blend for 30 seconds. Scrape down the sides of blender; blend for 1 minute. Refrigerate for 1 hour.

Meanwhile, make the sauce. Heat oil in large skillet. Brown the meat and onion, stirring frequently. Drain off excess fat. Add chili powder, cumin, salt, pepper, and tomato sauce; simmer for 20 minutes. Keep sauce warm while making crepes.

Heat lightly oiled skillet or small crepe pan over moderate heat until a drop of water sizzles and dances on the hot pan. Stir the batter. Pour a scant ¼ cup batter into pan and tilt pan in all directions to coat the bottom. Cook until bottom is lightly browned and the edges appear dry. Turn; cook a few seconds, until lightly browned. Stack on a towel, with paper towels between each. Keep crepes warm in oven as others are cooked. When all crepes are made, fill each with some meat mixture; roll crepes, and place on warm platter.

Garnish enchiladas with fresh tomato wedges and parsley. Makes 6 servings.

leg of lamb mexican-style
pierna de carnero a la mexicana

2 cloves garlic
1 tablespoon dried oregano
⅛ teaspoon ground cumin
2 teaspoons chili powder
1 4- to 5-pound leg of lamb
Salt and pepper
2 tablespoons wine vinegar
3 tablespoons olive oil
1 onion, chopped

Peel garlic; mash with oregano and cumin. Add a few drops of water, so that mixture forms a stiff paste. Stir in chili powder.

Wipe leg of lamb with damp cloth. With sharp knife make incisions all over surface of lamb. Put some spice mixture in each incision. Rub roast with salt and pepper.

Combine vinegar, olive oil, and onion.

Put roast in large plastic bag; pour oil and vinegar mixture over roast. Tie bag shut; marinate roast overnight.

Bring roast to room temperature. Roast lamb in open pan at 325°F for 30 minutes per pound.

Serve lamb with pan-roasted potatoes. Makes 8 to 10 servings.

lamb chops
mexican-style
*chuletas de carnero a
la mexicana*

4 large shoulder lamb chops
(about 1½ pounds total)
4 tablespoons olive oil
2 tablespoons lime juice
1 clove garlic, crushed
2 tablespoons grated onion
¼ cup flour
Salt and pepper
¼ cup lard
½ cup sherry

Wipe chops with a damp cloth; pat dry.

Combine olive oil, lime juice, garlic, and onion; rub into chops.
Refrigerate for several hours. Drain chops.

Combine flour and salt and pepper to taste. Dredge chops, shaking off
excess flour.

Heat lard in heavy skillet. Brown chops well on all sides over moderate
heat. Reduce heat to very low; cook for 20 minutes. Remove to warm
platter. Slowly pour sherry into pan, scraping browned bits from bottom
and sides of pan. Cook, stirring, several minutes. Pour sauce over the
chops, and serve. Makes 4 servings.

mexican
lamb
carnero a la mexicana

4 cups milk
1 onion, chopped
2 bay leaves
½ teaspoon dried thyme
1 teaspoon salt
¼ teaspoon pepper
¼ cup butter
2 pounds lamb, trimmed well
and cut into cubes
4 cups cooked rice
½ cup raisins (cook with the
rice)
½ cup sliced canned peaches
½ cup sliced canned pears
½ cup toasted sliced almonds
2 tablespoons fresh parsley

Combine milk, onion, bay leaves, thyme, salt, and pepper. Heat mixture,
but do not boil.

Heat butter in a skillet; sauté lamb until golden.

Add lamb to hot milk. Simmer uncovered over low heat until lamb is
tender and milk has cooked away (about 1 hour or more).

Place lamb in center of serving dish that has been covered with the hot
rice and raisin mixture. Arrange sliced peaches and pears around the
lamb. Sprinkle the lamb with almonds and parsley. Makes 4 to 6
servings.

mexican pork roast cooked in beer with green sauce

*lomo de puerco en cerveza
con salsa verde
a la mexicana*

2 medium onions, chopped
2 carrots, peeled and sliced
1 4- to 5-pound loin or
  shoulder pork roast

2 teaspoons salt
½ teaspoon oregano
½ teaspoon ground coriander
½ to ¾ cup beer

Place onions and carrots in roasting pan.

Rub pork with salt, oregano, and coriander. Place pork on top of vegetables; add beer. Cover; roast at 350°F for 2¾ hours. Add more beer, if necessary.

Slice and serve pork with Hot Dip (see Index) or Green Sauce and rice and Refried Beans (see Index).

Note: This may be cooked in a slow cooker on a low setting with 2 cups of beer for 8 to 12 hours.

green sauce

2 tablespoons olive oil
1 medium onion, chopped
1 clove garlic, peeled and
  chopped
1 10-ounce can Mexican green
  tomatoes (tomatillos)

½ teaspoon crumbled dried
  oregano
½ teaspoon dried cilantro
2 tablespoons wine vinegar
Salt and pepper

Heat olive oil in small skillet. Sauté onion and garlic until limp. Drain tomatillos; reserve liquid. In jar of electric blender combine tomatillos, ½ cup reserved liquid, onion, garlic, and olive oil, oregano, and cilantro; puree.

Heat skillet once again over moderate heat. Pour in sauce; cook for 10 minutes. Remove from heat; add wine vinegar and salt and pepper to taste.

Chill sauce and serve with meat dishes. Makes 6 to 8 servings.

pork chops with rice

puerco con arroz

4 loin pork chops, about 1½
  pounds total
3 tablespoons olive oil
1 medium onion, chopped
1 clove garlic, minced
1 green pepper, seeded and
  chopped
1 cup raw long-grain rice

2 cups boiling water
2 tablespoons dry sherry
2 teaspoons chicken-broth
  granules
2 packs cilantro and achiote
  seasoning mix (5 grams
  each)
½ cup sliced black olives

Sauté pork chops in olive oil in large, heavy skillet until well-browned. Remove from skillet. Add onion, garlic, and pepper; sauté over medium heat until limp. Add rice; sauté until lightly browned.

Combine boiling water, chicken-broth granules, cilantro and achiote seasoning mix, and sherry. Pour over rice. Top with pork chops; cover. Reduce heat to low; cook for 20 to 25 minutes or until all liquid is absorbed.

Top the chops with the sliced olives, and serve. Makes 4 servings.

Note: Cilantro and achiote seasoning mix is sold in Latin American and Carribbean markets and is sometimes referred to as Creole seasoning. If you cannot obtain it, substitute 2 tablespoons tomato paste and ½ teaspoon ground cumin for the seasoning mix.

41

pork spareribs in mexican barbecue sauce

barbacoa de costillas de puerco

mexican barbecue sauce
1 tablespoon olive oil
1 medium onion, chopped
1 clove garlic, peeled and minced
1 fresh chili pepper, stemmed, seeded, and chopped
½ tablespoon salt

2 large tomatoes, peeled and cut up
2 tablespoons chili powder
2 tablespoons sugar
¼ cup vinegar
⅓ cup olive oil
¼ cup beer

4 pounds pork spareribs (country-style)

First make the sauce. Heat the tablespoon of olive oil in saucepan. Sauté onion in oil until lightly browned. Add garlic, chopped chili, salt, and tomatoes; simmer until mixture thickens. Add remaining sauce ingredients; cook for 8 minutes, stirring constantly.

Marinate spareribs in sauce for several hours before grilling (if possible).

Grill over hot charcoal, basting periodically with sauce, until tender, well-browned, and crusty.

Pour extra sauce on the ribs before serving. Makes 6 to 8 servings.

mexican sausage

chorizo

This sausage mix keeps well in a glass jar in the refrigerator, or it may be frozen. Use in chili or taco filling or substitute it for purchased chorizo sausage in the recipes in this book.

1 pound lean pork shoulder
2 tablespoons vinegar
1 teaspoon crushed oregano
1 clove garlic, mashed
2 tablespoons chili powder

½ teaspoon freshly ground black pepper
1 teaspoon salt
⅛ teaspoon ground cumin

Coarsely grind pork shoulder. Add vinegar, oregano, garlic, chili powder, pepper, salt, and cumin. Mix thoroughly with your hands. Pack into crock or glass jar; store in refrigerator up to 2 weeks, or freeze. Makes 1 pound of sausage meat or the equivalent of 5 purchased chorizo links.

Use ⅓ cup of the mixture for each commercial sausage link called for in a recipe.

rabbit in wine sauce

conejo en vinado

4 pounds rabbit, cut in serving-size pieces
Seasoned flour
Oil for frying
1 onion, minced
1 green pepper, chopped
2 cloves garlic, minced
1 tablespoon dried parsley
¼ cup chopped celery

¼ cup catsup
1 tablespoon chili powder
½ cup broth
1½ cups Burgundy
Salt and pepper to taste
2 tablespoons chopped raisins
2 tablespoons chopped green olives
½ cup finely ground filberts

Coat rabbit with seasoned flour. Brown in hot oil. Remove from pan. Drain excess fat. Fry onion, pepper, garlic, parsley, and celery until soft but not browned. Add catsup and chili powder, which have been dissolved in broth. Add wine; season with salt and pepper to taste. Simmer for 10 minutes. Add rabbit; continue cooking for 30 to 40 minutes, until tender. Then add raisins, olives, and filberts. Makes 6 servings.

pork kebabs yucatan

This dish is especially good charcoal-grilled.

Juice of 1 lime
¼ cup salad oil
¼ teaspoon crushed whole
  coriander
¼ cup chopped onion
1 clove garlic, mashed
¼ teaspoon pepper

1¼ pounds lean pork, cut in
  1½-inch cubes
1 medium zucchini, sliced
2 red peppers, stemmed,
  seeded, and cut in chunks
½ pound mushrooms, cleaned
  and stems cut off

The day before cooking combine lime juice, oil, coriander, onion, garlic, and pepper in a glass or pottery bowl or casserole. Add meat; stir to coat with marinade. Cover; refrigerate 24 hours, stirring once or twice.

To cook, drain meat, reserving marinade. Skewer meat alternately with zucchini, red peppers, and mushrooms. Broil until done through (20 to 25 minutes), basting occasionally with marinade.

Serve kebabs with cooked rice. Makes 4 servings.

pork kebabs yucatan

pork in red chili sauce

puerco en salsa chile rojo

2 tablespoons lard (optional)
1 medium onion, chopped
1 clove garlic, minced
1½ to 2 tablespoons chili powder
1½ pounds lean pork, cut into 1½-inch cubes (reserve the fat)

1½ cups canned tomatoes, broken up with a fork
½ teaspoon salt
½ teaspoon crumbled oregano
½ teaspoon ground cumin
⅛ teaspoon ground cloves
1 small cinnamon stick

Render strips of pork fat or heat lard in Dutch oven over moderate heat. Remove strips of fat, if used; add onion and garlic, and brown lightly. Add chili powder; stir well. Push vegetables to sides of pan; brown meat on all sides. Add tomatoes, salt, oregano, cumin, cloves, and cinnamon stick. Stir well; bring to a boil. Reduce heat to low, cover, and cook for 2 hours or until meat is very tender. Stir mixture occasionally while it is cooking. If sauce is quite thin, cook uncovered the last 15 to 20 minutes of cooking.

Serve pork with rice and tortillas. Makes 4 servings.

veal with mexican sauce

ternero con salsa mexicano

mexican sauce

2 cups chopped peeled tomatoes or 1 16-ounce can whole tomatoes and juice
1 small onion, chopped
1 clove garlic, chopped

1 green pepper, chopped
1 tablespoon chili powder
½ teaspoon oregano
1 teaspoon salt
Few drops of hot sauce

4 cubed veal steaks
2 eggs, beaten
1 cup dry bread crumbs

Salt and pepper
½ cup butter
½ cup shredded Jack cheese

Combine all sauce ingredients in blender container; blend until smooth. Pour into small saucepan; simmer for 30 minutes. Makes 2½ to 3 cups sauce.

Dip veal in beaten eggs. Coat with bread crumbs, salt, and pepper. Fry in butter until browned; drain. Put veal in pan, cover with sauce, and top with shredded cheese. Bake at 350°F for 20 minutes. Makes 4 servings.

rice with veal and sour cream

arroz con ternera y jocoqui

1½ pounds veal, cut into small pieces
2 tablespoons oil
1 medium onion, chopped
1 clove garlic, minced
1 medium green pepper, chopped

2 tablespoons minced parsley
1 teaspoon paprika
3 cups beef broth
1 cup uncooked rice
1 cup sour cream
Salt and pepper to taste

Brown the veal in oil. Add onion, garlic, and green pepper. Cook for a few minutes. Add parsley, paprika, and broth. Simmer, covered, for 15 minutes. Add rice, stir, cover, and cook an additional 15 minutes. Slowly stir in sour cream, season to taste, cover, and cook 15 minutes longer. Serve rice hot. Makes 4 to 6 servings.

poultry

chicken cooked with corn
pollo con elote

1 2½- to 3-pound broiler-fryer chicken	*sauce*
4 tablespoons butter or margarine	3 tablespoons butter or margarine
Salt and pepper	2 tablespoons flour
1 16½-ounce can whole-kernel corn, drained, and the liquid reserved	1 cup half and half
	2 eggs, separated
	Salt and white pepper
½ cup chopped green chilies (optional)	¼ teaspoon nutmeg
	2 tablespoons bread crumbs
	2 tablespoons butter

Wash chicken, pat dry, and cut into quarters.

Heat butter or margarine in heavy skillet. Brown chicken on all sides. Place in an ovenproof casserole. Season chicken with salt and pepper to taste. Add corn and chilies (if used) to juices in skillet along with ¼ cup reserved corn liquid. Stir well; pour over chicken.

Next make the sauce. Melt butter or margarine in saucepan. Add flour; cook until evenly and lightly browned, stirring constantly. Add half and half all at once; cook over medium heat, stirring, until slightly thickened.

Beat egg yolks, salt, pepper, and nutmeg together. Add some hot sauce to egg yolks; beat well. Pour egg-yolk mixture into saucepan; mix well. Remove from the heat.

Beat egg whites until stiff but not dry; fold into sauce. Pour sauce over chicken, sprinkle with bread crumbs, and dot with butter. Bake in a preheated 350°F oven for 45 minutes. Makes 4 servings.

tablecloth stainer
mancha manteles

Tablecloth stainer is the literal translation, and believe me it does!

2 tablespoons butter or
   margarine
2 tablespoons cooking oil
1 pound boneless pork, cut
   into 1-inch chunks

1 roasting chicken (4 to 5
   pounds), disjointed
½ cup flour

sauce

1 tablespoon blanched,
   slivered almonds
2 teaspoons sesame seeds
1 medium onion, chopped

1 green pepper, seeded and
   chopped
1 16-ounce can tomatoes,
   broken up with a fork

2 cups chicken stock
½ cup white wine
¼ cup sugar
1½ teaspoons cinnamon
1 tablespoon chili powder
3 cloves
1 bay leaf

1 sweet potato, peeled and cut
   into cubes
1 medium apple
1 cup pineapple chunks,
   drained
2 medium bananas (optional)

Heat butter and oil together in Dutch oven. Sauté pork until well-browned.

Dredge chicken in flour; brown well. Reserve meats while making sauce.

Add 1 tablespoon of oil to pan, if necessary. Sauté almonds, sesame seeds, onion, and pepper until lightly browned. Add tomatoes; simmer for 10 minutes. Puree sauce in blender.

In Dutch oven combine pureed sauce, chicken stock, wine, sugar, cinnamon, chili powder, cloves, and bay leaf. Add chicken and pork. Bring to a boil. Reduce heat to low; cook for 30 minutes. Add sweet potato; cook 15 minutes more.

Peel, core, and dice apple. Add apple and pineapple to stew; heat through.

Serve stew in bowls. Peel and slice bananas into individual bowls as the stew is served. Makes 6 servings.

chicken and taco chips casserole
pollo y totopos en cazuela

9 taco shells or 1 12-ounce bag
   taco chips
2 whole chicken breasts,
   cooked and chopped
1 10½-ounce can chicken and
   rice soup

2 cups grated sharp cheddar
   cheese
1 10-ounce can tomatoes and
   green chilies

Crush taco chips in a bowl. Place a layer of crushed chips in bottom of greased 1-quart casserole. Sprinkle a layer of chopped chicken over chips. Pour several spoonfuls of condensed chicken and rice soup over the chicken layer. Sprinkle with a layer of grated cheese. Pour several spoonfuls of tomato and green chili mixture over cheese layer. Repeat process of layering chips, chicken, soup, cheese, and chilies until all ingredients are used. Top casserole with additional grated cheese if desired. Bake for 25 minutes at 350°F.

This may be prepared ahead and refrigerated before baking. It freezes well before and after baking. Makes 4 to 6 servings.

chicken with rice

pollo con arroz

2½ to 3 pounds fryer chicken
   parts
5 tablespoons butter or
   margarine
4 tablespoons olive oil
2 tablespoons sherry
1 small onion, chopped
1 green pepper, chopped
1 clove garlic, minced
1 cup raw long-grain rice
1½ cups chicken broth
1 bay leaf
½ teaspoon salt
¼ teaspoon pepper
Pinch of saffron
2 medium tomatoes, peeled
   and sliced
2 tablespoons Parmesan
   cheese

Wash chicken; pat dry.

Heat 4 tablespoons each butter and oil in large skillet over moderate heat. Brown chicken well on all sides. Pour sherry over chicken; remove chicken from pan. Add onion, green pepper, and garlic; sauté until golden. Add rice; sauté for 2 minutes. Add chicken broth, bay leaf, salt, pepper, and saffron. Bring mixture to a boil.

Grease 2-quart casserole. Pour in rice mixture; top with chicken. Cover casserole; bake at 350°F for 45 minutes.

Sauté tomatoes in remaining 1 tablespoon butter; place on chicken. Sprinkle with cheese; bake 15 more minutes.

Serve from the casserole with salad and bread. Makes 4 servings.

chicken with orange juice

pollo con jugo de naranja

1½ pounds chicken breasts,
   split (4 chicken pieces total)
½ cup flour
½ teaspoon salt
¼ teaspoon pepper
¼ cup vegetable oil
¼ cup sherry or golden rum
½ cup crushed pineapple in
   natural juice
¾ cup orange juice
¼ cup seedless raisins
¼ teaspoon ground cinnamon
⅛ teaspoon ground cloves
2 tablespoons butter
¼ cup blanched slivered
   almonds

Rinse chicken; pat dry.

Combine flour, salt, and pepper. Dredge chicken breasts thoroughly, shaking off excess flour.

Heat oil over moderate heat in heavy skillet. Brown the chicken pieces on all sides until golden. Place chicken pieces in shallow pan.

Combine the sherry, pineapple, orange juice, raisins, cinnamon, and cloves. Pour mixture over chicken. Bake uncovered at 350°F for 30 minutes, basting frequently.

In a small saucepan melt the butter. Add the almonds and sauté over moderate heat until golden. Pour the almonds and butter over the chicken. Serve chicken with rice. Makes 4 servings.

company chicken and rice casserole

pollo y arroz especial

3 tablespoons olive oil
½ cup chopped onion
1 cup raw long-grain rice
2 cups chicken broth
3 tablespoons dry sherry
1 bay leaf
Salt and pepper

1 teaspoon dried cilantro
  (dried coriander leaves)
2 cups cooked chicken, boned,
  skinned, and shredded
¾ cup sour cream
½ cup sliced stuffed green
  olives

Heat oil in large, heavy skillet. Sauté onion until limp. Add rice; cook, stirring occasionally, until lightly browned. Add chicken broth, sherry, bay leaf, salt and pepper to taste, cilantro, and chicken. Stir well. Bring mixture to a boil. Cover, reduce heat to simmer, and cook for 20 minutes or until all liquid is absorbed. Uncover; stir in sour cream. Over very low heat, cook just long enough to heat through.

Top chicken with the sliced olives, and serve. Makes 4 servings.

sour-cream chicken enchiladas

enchiladas de pollo en jocoqui

enchilada sauce
1 clove garlic, minced
2 small onions, chopped
3 tablespoons oil
2 tablespoons flour
1¾ cups chicken bouillon
2 5-ounce cans green chilies,
  drained and chopped
2 cups canned tomatoes,
  drained well and chopped
  (2 28-ounce cans)

enchiladas
12 corn tortillas, fresh or
  frozen (thawed)
1 pint sour cream
½ pound New York White
  Cheddar, shredded
4 cups cooked and shredded
  chicken
Extra cheese (shredded) and
  black olive slices for
  topping (if desired)

To make the sauce, sauté garlic and onions in oil. Add flour; stir in bouillon. Cook, stirring constantly, about 5 minutes, until thickened. Add chilies and tomatoes; allow to simmer for 5 to 10 minutes. Makes 3½ to 4 cups of sauce.

To assemble the enchiladas, dip tortillas in hot oil to soften. Drain well on paper towels. Mix sour cream, shredded cheese, and chicken. Place filling in center of each tortilla; roll them up. Use approximately ½ cup filling per tortilla. Place rolled enchiladas side-by-side in a large baking dish; pour sauce over them. Sprinkle with extra cheese and sliced black olives if desired. Bake at 350°F for about 30 minutes, until bubbly and hot. Makes 6 servings (2 enchiladas each).

mexican chicken livers
hígados de pollo mexicana

1 pound chicken livers
½ cup flour
½ teaspoon salt
⅛ teaspoon pepper
6 tablespoons butter
5 scallions, sliced
½ pound fresh mushrooms, sliced
¼ cup sherry (more as desired)

Coat chicken livers with flour mixed with salt and pepper.

Melt butter; sauté chicken livers until golden brown. Add scallions and mushrooms; cook until tender. Add desired amount of sherry; simmer for 5 minutes.

Serve livers on toast or rice. Makes 4 servings.

open-faced tortilla sandwiches
tostadas

sauce
½ cup onion
2 tablespoons olive oil
1½ cups drained and cut-up canned tomatoes
3 tablespoons chopped canned green chilies
2 tablespoons chopped cilantro
(2 4-ounce cans taco sauce may be substituted for the sauce)

tostadas
Vegetable oil for frying
8 corn tortillas (6 to 7 inches in diameter)
2 cups Refried Beans (see Index)
1½ cups grated Jack cheese
3 cups cubed cooked chicken breast
3 cups shredded iceberg lettuce
1 large ripe avocado
2 tablespoons lemon juice

First make the sauce. Sauté onion in hot oil until lightly browned. Add tomatoes and chilies; cook over low heat until thick. Add cilantro; cool.

To assemble the tostadas, heat oil over moderate heat in heavy 8-inch frying pan until quite hot. Fry tortillas, one at a time, flat, until crisp; drain on paper towels. Spread tortillas with beans; sprinkle with cheese, chicken, and lettuce. Peel and slice avocado. Dip slices in lemon juice; place on top of tostadas.

Top with sauce. Serve. Makes 4 servings.

Alternately: Spread tortillas with beans and serve the rest of the ingredients in small bowls on the table so that each person can assemble his own *tostada.*

chicken with tomatoes and olives

pollo con salsa de tomate y aceituna

4 breast quarters of frying
  chicken
½ cup flour
2 tablespoons butter
2 tablespoons olive oil
1 clove garlic, chopped
1 cup chopped onion
¼ cup chopped carrots
¼ cup chopped celery
2 cups broken-up canned
  tomatoes
½ cup white wine
1 teaspoon chili powder
½ teaspoon ground cumin
½ teaspoon salt
¼ teaspoon pepper
¾ cup cut-up black olives

Wash chicken; pat dry. Dredge chicken in flour, shaking off excess.

Heat butter and oil together in deep skillet or Dutch oven. Brown chicken well on all sides. Remove chicken from pan. Lightly brown garlic, onion, carrots, and celery in pan drippings.

Force tomatoes through a sieve, or puree in blender. Add tomatoes and wine to vegetables in pan or skillet. Add the seasonings; stir well. Place chicken in sauce. Simmer over low heat 30 minutes or until chicken is tender. Add olives; heat through.

Serve chicken with rice, crusty bread, and a green salad. Makes 4 servings.

chicken cooked in foil

pollo en camisa

1 2½- to 3-pound chicken
2 tablespoons olive oil
Salt and pepper
1 medium onion, finely
  chopped
1 clove garlic, minced
¼ cup chopped green chilies
2 tablespoons chopped fresh
  cilantro (or 2 teaspoons
  dried cilantro)
2 fresh tomatoes, peeled and
  chopped

Wash chicken, drain, and pat dry. Cut chicken into quarters.

Cut 4 10-inch squares of heavy-duty foil. Divide oil among the 4 sheets of foil. Grease foil. Place a chicken piece on each foil sheet; grease. Salt and pepper chicken to taste.

Combine onion, garlic, chilies, cilantro, and tomatoes in small bowl. Spoon some sauce over each piece of chicken; fold foil into a neat, sealed package. Place on cookie sheet; bake at 425°F for 40 minutes. Carefully open foil packages and allow steam to escape.

Serve from the foil packages with a crisp green salad. Makes 4 servings.

chicken with tomatoes and olives

chicken cooked in foil

fiesta turkey in mole sauce

salsa mole poblano de guajolote

Turkey with Mole Sauce is the most popular fiesta dish of Mexico! It is a must during the Christmas season. The dish was originally concocted by the nuns of an isolated convent who had no special dinner for the visiting archbishop. The nuns killed their only turkey and made a special sauce with all the interesting ingredients in their kitchen. The result was this heavenly dish!

1 10- to 12-pound turkey,
   disjointed
¼ cup cooking oil
1 teaspoon salt
Water

mole sauce
6 dried Ancho chilies
Boiling water
2 tablespoons oil
1 medium onion, chopped
2 cloves garlic, minced
½ teaspoon crushed chilies
1 cup chopped canned Italian
   plum tomatoes
¾ teaspoon ground cinnamon
½ teaspoon ground cloves
¼ teaspoon ground coriander
¼ teaspoon anise
¼ teaspoon cumin
1 dry tortilla, cut into pieces
¼ cup sesame seeds
¼ cup raisins
2 cups chicken broth
2 squares (1 ounce each)
   semisweet chocolate, grated

Wash turkey; pat dry.

Heat oil in Dutch oven; brown the turkey well on all sides, adding more oil if necessary to keep the turkey from sticking. Add salt and enough water to cover. Bring to a boil. Cover; reduce heat to low. Cook 1 hour or until tender. Set aside.

Meanwhile, prepare the sauce. Stem and seed red chilies under cold running water. Tear chilies into pieces; soak in boiling water to cover for 30 minutes. Drain; reserve ¼ cup soaking liquid.

Heat oil in skillet. Sauté onion and garlic until limp.

In blender jar combine Ancho chilies, reserved liquid, onion, garlic, crushed chilies, tomatoes, and spices; puree until smooth. Add tortilla, sesame seeds, and raisins; puree, scraping blender container frequently.

Heat skillet in which onion was cooked over moderate heat for several minutes. Pour puree into skillet; add chicken broth, stirring well. Simmer for 10 minutes. Remove from heat and add chocolate. Stir until chocolate melts.

Drain broth from turkey. Pour sauce over turkey; heat through.

Serve turkey garnished with sesame seeds. Makes 8 to 10 servings.

Note: The turkey could be roasted unstuffed, sliced, and served with the mole sauce if you prefer. Mole sauce is a long and complicated business. It is available in Latin American grocery stores and specialty stores canned and as a powder. It is reconstituted with broth before serving. Chicken and pork are also served with this sauce.

braised duck in green mole sauce

pato en salsa mole verde

1 5- to 6-pound duckling
1 clove garlic, mashed
¾ teaspoon salt
½ teaspoon pepper
3 tablespoons butter or
　margarine

green mole sauce
3 tablespoons olive oil
1 slice white bread
½ cup raw shelled pumpkin
　seeds (raw pepitas)
¼ cup blanched slivered
　almonds
1 10-ounce can Mexican green
　tomatoes (tomatillos)
1 4-ounce can peeled green
　chilies
3 tablespoons chopped
　cilantro
1½ cups chicken broth
Salt and pepper

Wash duck, clean thoroughly, and pat dry. Singe any pinfeathers. Rub with garlic, salt, and pepper.

In large Dutch oven or stove-top casserole, heat butter or margarine over moderate heat until lightly browned. Brown duck well on all sides, pricking to release some fat from duck. Cover, reduce heat to low, and cook without liquid 25 to 35 minutes or until done through.

Meanwhile, make the sauce. Heat 2 tablespoons oil in skillet; fry bread until golden brown on both sides. Drain on paper towels.

Add remaining oil to skillet; brown pumpkin seeds and almonds. Drain.

Drain green tomatoes.

Seed and chop green chilies.

Combine green tomatoes, fried bread (torn into pieces), nuts and seeds, green chilies, cilantro, ½ cup chicken broth, and salt and pepper; puree.

Heat skillet over moderate heat. Pour sauce into skillet; stir in remaining chicken broth. Simmer for 5 to 10 minutes.

Carve the duck and serve topped with the sauce. Makes 3 to 4 servings.

fish

poached fish with avocado sauce
pescado con salsa de aguacate

1½ to 2 pounds frozen fish
   fillets, thawed
2 onions, thinly sliced
2 lemons, thinly sliced
2 tablespoons butter, melted
2 teaspoons salt
1 bay leaf
½ teaspoon black pepper
3 cups water
1 lemon (cut in half—squeeze
   1 half, slice other half)

avocado sauce
2 mashed avocados
½ cup sour cream
2 tablespoons lemon juice
½ small onion, finely chopped

Cut fillets into serving portions.

Combine onions and lemon slices with butter, salt, bay leaf, and black pepper in an ovenproof baking dish. Place fillets on top of onion and lemon slices; add the water. Cover; cook at 350°F for 45 minutes.

Before serving, carefully remove fish fillets with slotted spoon or spatula. Place on heated platter. Sprinkle with juice from ½ lemon. Garnish with additional lemon slices.

Prepare Avocado Sauce by mixing all sauce ingredients well.

Serve the hot fish with the sauce, or chill the fish and serve it cold. Makes 6 servings.

fried fish with sour sauce
escabeche de pescado frito

Escabeche literally means "cooked with sour sauce." The dish is of Spanish heritage and can feature meat or fowl in place of fish.

1 pound firm white fish, cut into steaks or fillets
¾ teaspoon salt
1 large onion, sliced
½ cup olive oil
1 clove garlic, minced
½ cup water
1 bay leaf
6 whole peppercorns
½ teaspoon toasted coriander seeds

1 egg, well-beaten
2 tablespoons water
¾ cup cornmeal
½ cup red wine vinegar
3 tablespoons olive oil
¼ cup sliced Spanish olives stuffed with pimientos
¼ cup chopped onion

Sprinkle fish with salt; let stand ½ hour.

Meanwhile, slowly fry onion in ½ cup olive oil in heavy frying pan. Do not brown. Add garlic; continue to fry for a few minutes. Remove onion and garlic from oil with a slotted spoon; place in a small saucepan. Add ½ cup water, bay leaf, peppercorns, and coriander; simmer while frying fish.

Beat egg and 2 tablespoons water together. Dip fish in egg wash, then in cornmeal, coating well. Fry in seasoned olive oil until well-browned. Drain on paper towels; place on warm platter.

Add vinegar and 3 tablespoons olive oil to onion and spice mixture. Remove bay leaf, peppercorns, and coriander seeds.

Pour the sauce over the fish and garnish with the sliced olives and chopped onion. Makes 4 servings.

fillet of sole acapulco-style
pescado acapulco

Acapulco, due to the international character of its many visitors, provides some of the best continental-style cuisine to be found anywhere, with its own special touches!

1 pound fresh spinach
1 tablespoon butter
1 tablespoon olive oil
1 clove garlic, minced
Salt and pepper
1 pound sole fillets

¼ cup butter or margarine
½ cup flour
Juice of ½ lemon
5 large slices fresh tomato
1 cup grated Edam cheese

Clean and wash spinach well. Remove all coarse stems; shake as much water as possible from leaves.

Heat 1 tablespoon each butter and oil in large skillet. Add garlic; sauté 2 minutes. Add spinach; immediately cover pan. Cook over high heat until steam appears. Reduce heat to low; simmer 5 minutes. Season with salt and pepper; turn into an 11 × 7 × 1¾-inch casserole dish.

Melt ¼ cup butter in skillet.

Dredge fish in flour; sauté in butter until browned. Drain; lay on top of spinach. Squeeze lemon juice over fish. Arrange tomato slices, overlapping on top of fish. Sprinkle with cheese; bake at 350°F for 20 to 25 minutes or until cheese is melted. Makes 4 servings.

red snapper a la veracruz

*huachinango
a la veracruzana*

1 to 1¼ pounds red-snapper
    fillets (4 fillets)
2 tablespoons lemon juice
Salt and pepper
2 tablespoons chopped capers
¼ cup sliced pimiento-stuffed
    green olives
2 tablespoons olive oil
½ cup chopped onion
1 clove garlic, minced
2 cups chopped canned
    tomatoes
¼ teaspoon crumbled thyme
¼ teaspoon crumbled
    marjoram
½ teaspoon crumbled oregano

Lightly oil small ovenproof baking dish, big enough to hold fish fillets in a single layer. Arrange fish in baking dish. Sprinkle with lemon juice; salt and pepper lightly. Sprinkle with capers and sliced olives.

Heat oil in small skillet. Add onion and garlic; cook until limp. Add tomatoes, thyme, marjoram, and oregano; simmer for 10 minutes. Pour over fish. Cover baking dish; bake at 350°F for 25 to 30 minutes or until fish flakes easily with a fork.

Serve fish with small, boiled new potatoes. Makes 4 servings.

fried fish with mexican sauce

*pescado frito con salsa
mexicano*

1 pound firm fish fillets,
    defrosted if frozen
    (flounder or sole)
2 tablespoons lemon juice

½ teaspoon salt
¼ teaspoon pepper
½ cup flour
¼ cup cooking oil

mexican sauce
2 tablespoons olive oil
1 small onion, chopped
½ cup chopped green pepper
¼ cup chopped celery
1 clove garlic, minced

1 cup drained and chopped
    canned peeled tomatoes
2 tablespoons dry sherry
Salt and pepper
1 large pinch saffron

2 tablespoons chopped parsley
    (for garnish)

Sprinkle fish fillets with lemon juice, salt and pepper; set aside while making the sauce.

Heat olive oil in saucepan or small skillet. Add onion, green pepper, celery, and garlic; sauté until limp. Add tomatoes, sherry, salt and pepper to taste, and saffron. Stir well; simmer while frying fish.

Drain fish well.

Heat cooking oil over moderate heat in large frying pan. Dip fish in flour, coating well; fry until golden, turning once.

Drain fish and serve hot, topped with the sauce. Garnish with chopped parsley. Makes 4 servings.

shrimp fritters

tortas de camarón

tomato sauce
2 tablespoons olive oil
1 medium onion, chopped
1 clove garlic, minced
1 10-ounce can tomatoes and
   green chilies
½ teaspoon salt
¼ teaspoon pepper

fritters
4 eggs, separated
½ teaspoon salt
¼ teaspoon celery salt
2 teaspoons dried parsley
   flakes
2 tablespoons flour
1 cup well-drained chopped
   cooked shrimp (fresh,
   frozen, or canned)
Oil for frying

First make the sauce; keep it warm while making fritters. Heat oil in medium saucepan. Add onion and garlic; sauté until limp. Add tomatoes and green chilies and seasonings. Bring to a boil. Reduce heat to simmer. Cover; cook for 20 minutes.

Meanwhile, beat egg whites until stiff.

Beat egg yolks, salt, celery salt, parsley flakes, and flour. Fold into egg whites. Fold shrimp into egg-white batter.

In heavy skillet or deep fryer heat at least 1 inch of oil to 365°F. Fry fritters a few at a time (using ¼ cup batter for each fritter) until golden. Drain well.

Serve fritters immediately with the Tomato Sauce. Makes 4 servings.

grilled shrimp with barbecue sauce

camarónes en parilla con salsa barbacoa

barbecue sauce
2 cups catsup
1 cup water
½ cup cider vinegar
¾ cup sugar
½ cup chopped onion
½ cup chopped green pepper
½ cup chopped celery
¼ cup chopped parsley
2 cloves garlic, minced
1 lemon, whole

1 pound medium shrimp (30
   to 32 count)
1½ cups barbecue sauce

⅛ teaspoon hot-pepper sauce
1½ tablespoons
   Worcestershire sauce
1½ tablespoons liquid smoke
1 teaspoon salt
½ teaspoon basil
½ teaspoon oregano
½ teaspoon cinnamon
2 tablespoons butter

¼ cup dry sherry or white
   wine
Heavy foil

In a pan combine catsup, water, vinegar, sugar, onion, pepper, celery, parsley, and garlic.

Squeeze juice from lemon, cut off ends, discard seeds; add rinds and juice to sauce. Add hot-pepper sauce, Worcestershire sauce, liquid smoke, salt, basil, oregano, cinnamon, and butter. Cook, uncovered, over medium heat, stirring often, until reduced to 1 quart—approximately 35 minutes. Cool, cover, and chill for storage up to 1 week. Makes 1 quart.

Clean 1 pound shrimp without removing shells. Wrap shrimp in heavy foil, pouring in 1½ cups Barbecue Sauce before sealing the packet. Refrigerate for 1 to 2 hours.

Place on grill, cover with the hood or with foil. Allow to cook 40 minutes. At this point, the shrimp should be tender enough to eat shell and all. Pour ¼ cup dry sherry or white wine into the shrimp packet.

Serve the shrimp hot. Makes 4 servings.

spanish seafood and rice
paella la mancha

1 2½- to 3-pound broiler-fryer
   chicken, cut up
¼ cup olive oil
1 cup water
3 tablespoons olive oil
1 medium onion, chopped
1 clove garlic, minced
1½ cups raw long-grain white
   rice
2 teaspoons chicken-broth
   granules
¼ cup white wine
⅛ teaspoon saffron
⅛ teaspoon cayenne
1 teaspoon salt
Boiling water
2 tomatoes, peeled and cut in
   quarters
½ cup finely chopped ham
2 cups fresh or frozen raw
   shrimp, peeled and
   deveined
1 10-ounce package frozen
   peas, thawed

Wash chicken and pat dry.

Heat ¼ cup oil in skillet; sauté chicken until well-browned on all sides. Add water. Reduce heat to low; cook 20 minutes. Cool chicken; reserve pan juices.

Heat 3 tablespoons oil in Dutch oven. Sauté onion and garlic until limp. Add rice; sauté until lightly browned.

In large measuring cup, combine chicken-broth granules, wine, saffron, cayenne pepper, and salt; add enough boiling water to make 3 cups liquid. Add liquid to Dutch oven along with chicken, tomatoes, ham, and shrimp. Stir well. Cover; bring just to a boil. Reduce heat to low; cook for 20 minutes. Add peas; cook 10 minutes more.

Serve seafood in a shallow casserole or paella pan. Makes 5 to 6 servings.

eggs and cheese

eggs with avocado sauce
huevos con salsa aguacates

8 eggs, hard-boiled and peeled
2 tablespoons butter
2 tablespoons minced onion
1 tablespoon flour
1 tablespoon minced green chili
½ cup milk
2 ripe avocados
½ teaspoon salt
2 tomatoes, cut in wedges

Keep eggs warm by placing them in hot water while preparing the sauce.

Melt butter; cook onion until limp. Add flour; cook until bubbly. Add green chili; mix well. Add milk; cook, stirring constantly, until thickened.

Puree avocados in blender; add with salt to sauce.

Drain and halve eggs.

Place 4 egg halves on each serving plate, top with some of the sauce, and garnish with tomatoes. Makes 4 servings.

ranch-style eggs
huevos rancheros

sauce
2 tablespoons olive oil
¼ cup chopped onion
1 clove garlic, minced
1 1-pound can tomatoes

2 tablespoons chopped green
   chilies
½ teaspoon dried cilantro
½ teaspoon salt

Oil for frying
4 tortillas
2 tablespoons butter

8 eggs
1 small ripe avocado

First prepare the sauce. Heat oil in small skillet; sauté onion and garlic until lightly browned. Add tomatoes, green chilies, cilantro, and salt; simmer until thick. Keep sauce warm while cooking eggs.

Heat 1 inch vegetable oil in small cast-iron skillet over moderate heat. Soft-fry tortillas 1 at a time until they are just beginning to crisp. Drain and keep them warm.

Melt butter in heavy skillet; fry eggs sunny-side-up to desired degree of doneness.

Put a tortilla on each plate. Top with 2 eggs and some of the sauce.

Peel and slice the avocado; garnish the eggs with it. Makes 4 servings.

eggs and sausage
huevos con chorizo

2 tablespoons oil
1 small onion, finely chopped
¼ pound chorizo, homemade
   (see Index) or commercial,
   with the casings removed
8 eggs, lightly beaten
Salt and pepper to taste
1 large tomato, peeled,
   seeded, and chopped

Heat oil in large heavy skillet. Fry onion in oil until lightly browned. Add chorizo, breaking it up with a fork as it cooks. Cook until chorizo is lightly browned. Add eggs, salt and pepper, and tomato; reduce heat to low. Stir well. Continue to cook as you would scrambled eggs, until eggs are set and fairly dry.

Serve with warm tortillas and sliced oranges with cinnamon sugar. Makes 4 servings.

scrambled eggs with zucchini sauce
huevos revueltos con salsa calabacitas

2 medium zucchini, sliced
   diagonally
5 tablespoons butter
1 8-ounce can tomato sauce
1 teaspoon seasoned salt
¼ teaspoon pepper

8 eggs
½ cup milk
1 cup shredded cheddar
   cheese
Chopped chives (for color)

Sauté zucchini in 2 tablespoons butter. Stir in tomato sauce, salt, and pepper. Simmer for 8 to 10 minutes.

Beat eggs with milk. Cook eggs in 3 tablespoons melted butter. When partially cooked, stir in ½ cup shredded cheese. Finish cooking.

Place servings of egg in individual dishes, with zucchini sauce on top. Sprinkle with chives and the remaining shredded cheese. Makes 4 servings.

mexican scrambled eggs

*huevos revueltos
a la mexicana*

8 eggs
2 tablespoons milk
1 large tomato, peeled,
   seeded, and chopped
1 tablespoon chopped green
   pepper
1 tablespoon chopped parsley
3 tablespoons butter
½ cup chopped ham
2 tablespoons chopped chives

Beat eggs in mixing bowl with milk. Add tomato, green pepper, and parsley; stir well to combine.

Melt butter over low heat in large, heavy skillet; sauté ham 3 minutes. Pour in egg mixture; cook, stirring frequently with a spatula, until set.

Sprinkle eggs with the chives and serve with hot, buttered tortillas for brunch. Makes 4 servings.

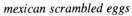

mexican scrambled eggs

spanish omelet

spanish omelet
tortilla de huevos a la español

sauce
2 tablespoons olive oil
1 small onion, chopped
1 clove garlic, peeled and
  chopped
2 green peppers, cleaned,
  seeded, and cut into strips

1 red pepper, cleaned, seeded,
  and cut into strips
1 8-ounce can tomato sauce
2 tablespoons dry sherry
½ teaspoon chili powder

omelets
2 tablespoons butter
6 eggs

First make the sauce. Heat oil in saucepan or skillet. Add onion, garlic, and peppers; cook until wilted. Add tomato sauce, sherry, and chili powder; keep sauce warm while making omelets.

In 8-inch skillet or omelet pan heat 1 tablespoon butter over medium heat until it starts to brown. Tilt pan in all directions to coat with butter.

Meanwhile, beat 3 eggs with a fork until yolks and whites are well-blended. Pour into skillet; cook over medium heat until set. Fold omelet, place on warm serving dish, and repeat procedure with remaining eggs and butter.

Serve topped with the sauce. Makes 4 to 6 servings.

stuffed chili with cheese casserole
chile rellenos con queso en cazuela

1 4-ounce can California green
  roasted chilies (or 4
  roasted, peeled Poblano
  chilies)
¼ pound sliced sharp cheddar
  cheese

4 eggs, separated
4 teaspoons flour
4 teaspoons water
1 teaspoon Beau Monde
¼ teaspoon salt

Lightly oil a 1½- to 2-quart glass or ceramic casserole; set aside.

Rinse and seed chilies. Fill chilies with cheese slices, folding and cutting cheese so that chili pepper completely encases cheese. Place in a single layer in bottom of oiled casserole.

Combine egg yolks, flour, water, and Beau Monde in a small mixing bowl; beat on low speed until well-blended.

In another small mixing bowl beat egg whites until foamy. Sprinkle with salt; continue beating until stiff but not dry. Fold egg-yolk mixture lightly but thoroughly into stiffly beaten egg whites. Pour batter over chilies; bake at 325°F for 40 minutes or until puffed and lightly browned.

Serve with heated stewed tomatoes with onion and green pepper or with the following sauce.

sauce

½ cup finely chopped onion
1 clove garlic, minced
1 tablespoon olive oil
2 tablespoons tomato paste
1 cup chopped canned peeled
  tomatoes
1 can chicken broth, regular
  strength

1 teaspoon sugar
½ teaspoon salt
1 teaspoon vinegar
1 tablespoon flour
1 tablespoon water

Sauté onion and garlic in oil in small saucepan until lightly browned. Add tomato paste and chopped tomatoes; stir well. Add broth, sugar, salt, and vinegar. Cook on very low heat 1 to 1½ hours or until tomatoes are soft.

Force through a sieve or whirl in blender until smooth. Return to saucepan and heat until almost boiling.

Combine flour and water to form a smooth paste. Slowly stir flour paste into tomato mixture. Simmer until thickened. Makes 4 servings.

tortilla omelet
tortilla con huevos

1 tortilla
3 tablespoons oil
3 eggs, well-beaten
2 tablespoons milk

Salt and pepper
1 green onion, finely chopped
3 tablespoons Queso Blanco
  (or Jack cheese)

Cut tortilla into eighths.

Heat oil over moderate heat in 8-inch skillet or omelet pan. Fry tortilla pieces briefly to a light golden color (not as crisp as tortilla chips).

Meanwhile, beat eggs, milk, salt and pepper to taste, and green onion together. Pour egg mixture over tortillas; immediately reduce heat to low. Cook as you would an omelet, lifting cooked egg and allowing uncooked egg mixture to flow to bottom of pan. When omelet is lightly browned and almost done, sprinkle with cheese; allow to melt. Fold or cut in wedges.

Serve omelet with fried Chorizo (see Index) and rolls. Makes 2 servings.

cheese enchiladas
enchiladas de queso

8 6-inch corn tortillas
Oil for frying
2½ cups grated sharp cheddar
  cheese
¾ cup chopped onion
1 6-ounce can ripe olives,
  drained and chopped

1 recipe Red Chili Sauce or 2
  10-ounce cans Enchilada
  Sauce
1 cup grated Jack cheese
Ripe olives

Soften tortillas in hot oil in small skillet until pliable (not crisp).

Combine cheese, onion, and olives; toss well to combine. Place heaping ½ cup cheese mixture in center of each tortilla; roll up to form a tubular shape. Place enchiladas side by side in ovenproof 13 × 9 × 2-inch pan. Top with Red Chili Sauce or Enchilada Sauce. Sprinkle with Jack cheese; garnish with additional black olives. Bake, uncovered, at 350°F for 30 minutes or until hot and bubbly. Makes 4 servings.

red chili sauce

½ cup chopped onion
1 clove garlic, minced
3 cups canned Italian plum
  tomatoes, drained
½ teaspoon salt

½ teaspoon oregano
2 tablespoons vegetable oil
3 tablespoons flour
3 tablespoons chili powder
1 cup water

Combine onion, garlic, tomatoes, salt, and oregano in jar of electric blender. Whirl until smooth.

Heat vegetable oil in small skillet. Add tomato mixture; simmer 20 minutes.

Combine flour and chili powder in large saucepan; add enough water to make a smooth paste. Slowly stir in cooked tomato puree and 1 cup water; combine well. Cook over moderate heat, stirring constantly, until thickened. Reduce heat to low; simmer 20 minutes.

mexican fondue

1 pound (4 cups) shredded
  cheddar cheese
1 pound (4 cups) shredded
  Monterey Jack cheese
¼ cup all-purpose flour
2 teaspoons chili powder
1 clove garlic, halved
1 12-ounce can beer
1 4-ounce can hot green chili
  peppers, seeded and
  chopped

Amounts as desired:
  French bread, cubed
  Cooked ham, cubed
  Cooked shrimp, peeled
  Cherry tomatoes
  Green pepper strips
  Avocado slices

Combine cheeses with flour and chili powder in large bowl until well-blended.

Rub the garlic half along the inside of a ceramic fondue pot; add beer and heat slowly, just until beer begins to bubble. Gradually add cheese mixture, a handful at a time, stirring constantly, until cheese has melted and is smooth; add hot peppers. Serve fondue warm.

Select desired dippers and arrange tray around fondue pot. Makes 8 servings.

rice with cheese
arroz con queso

2 cups sour cream
2 teaspoons salt
1 4-ounce can chopped green
   chilies

3 cups cooked long-grain rice
2½ cups shredded Jack cheese
½ cup grated sharp cheddar
   cheese

Thoroughly combine sour cream, salt, and chilies.

Grease a 1½-quart casserole. Layer one-fourth of rice, one-third of sour-cream mixture, and one-third of shredded Jack cheese in casserole. Continue layering until all ingredients are used, ending with a layer of rice. Sprinkle with cheddar cheese; bake at 350°F for 30 minutes. Makes 6 servings.

Note: If you like your Mexican food really hot, increase the amount of green chilies used.

tortilla and cheese casserole
chilaquiles

½ cup chopped onion
1 clove garlic, peeled and
   minced
2 tablespoons olive oil
1 10-ounce can Mexican green
   tomatoes (tomatillos)
2 jalapeño peppers, stemmed
   and seeded
1 teaspoon dried cilantro
1 teaspoon salt
¼ teaspoon pepper
½ teaspoon sugar
12 tortillas, cut in ½-inch
   strips
Oil or lard for frying
1 pound Monterey Jack
   cheese, grated
½ cup heavy cream

Sauté onion and garlic in olive oil until limp.

Drain tomatillos, reserving liquid.

In jar of electric blender combine tomatillos and ½ cup of reserved liquid, the jalapeño peppers, cilantro, salt, pepper, and sugar; whirl until smooth. Add to onions and garlic in skillet; simmer 10 minutes.

Heat 2 to 3 tablespoons oil or lard in skillet and fry tortilla strips a few at a time on both sides, without browning. Drain on paper towels. Add more fat to skillet as needed while frying tortillas.

Grease 2-quart casserole. Arrange a layer of tortilla strips on bottom of casserole. Top with a layer of sauce and a layer of cheese. Continue layering until all ingredients are used, ending with a layer of cheese. Pour heavy cream over top; bake at 350°F for 35 minutes. Makes 6 servings.

Note: If tomatillos are unavailable, use 2 cups of canned tomatoes and substitute cheddar cheese for the Jack cheese. Omit the heavy cream. Serve topped with sour cream.

vegetables

beans and corn
frijoles y maíz

½ pound black beans
4 cups cold water
1 onion, peeled and chopped
¼ pound salt pork, diced
1 teaspoon salt

1 16½-ounce can whole-kernel corn, drained
1 sprig fresh mint (optional)
Several dashes Tabasco

Wash beans; pick over well. Soak beans overnight in 4 cups cold water.
The following day add water to cover beans, if necessary. Add onion, salt pork, and salt to beans. Bring to a boil, reduce heat to low, and cook until beans are tender. Add corn and mint. Add Tabasco to taste; heat through. Makes 6 servings.

refried black beans
frijoles negroes refritos

¼ pound bulk chorizo sausage
¼ pound lard
1 recipe Beans in Savory
  Sauce (see Index)
½ cup Queso Blanco (or Jack
  cheese)
½ cup chopped onion

Fry chorizo in large, heavy skillet until lightly browned. Add lard; melt it. Add beans slowly (a cup at a time) while mashing with potato masher to form a thick paste. Fry over low heat, stirring and mashing occasionally, until thick and crusty. Top with cheese; melt cheese.

Roll beans onto a platter and top with onion. Serve with tortillas or tostadas. Makes 6 servings.

green beans with lime juice

ejotes con jugo de limón

2½ cups fresh or frozen green beans, cut into ¾-inch lengths
2 tablespoons butter
2 tablespoons parsley
½ teaspoon salt
¼ teaspoon pepper
1 tablespoon lime juice

Cook beans in boiling salted water until tender. Drain well.

Melt butter in heavy skillet. Add beans, parsley, salt, and pepper. Cook, stirring constantly, for 5 minutes. Add lime juice. Mix well; serve immediately. Makes 4 servings.

lima beans and peppers

habas verdes y chiles

1 10-ounce package frozen baby lima beans
3 tablespoons olive oil
½ cup green pepper, cut into thin strips
¼ cup sweet red pepper, cut into thin strips
¼ cup finely chopped onion

Cook beans in boiling salted water, according to package directions. Drain; keep them warm.

Heat oil in small skillet. Add green pepper, red pepper, and onion; sauté for 5 minutes.

Combine lima bean and pepper mixture gently. Serve immediately. Makes 4 servings.

lima beans and peppers

beans in savory sauce
frijoles en olla

1 pound black beans (*frijoles negroes*)
Water
2 teaspoons salt

savory sauce
2 tablespoons lard or olive oil
½ cup chopped onion
1 clove garlic, minced
2 pickled jalapeño peppers, seeded and finely chopped (Jalapeños en Escabeche)
1 large tomato, peeled, seeded, and chopped
1 teaspoon crushed marjoram
1 teaspoon crushed oregano
Salt and pepper to taste

Chopped onions for topping

Wash and pick over beans. Place in large saucepan; cover with water. Add salt; cook over low heat, replenishing water so that beans are always just covered. Cook at least 4 hours or until beans are very tender and mixture is thick.

Heat lard or oil in small skillet over moderate heat. Add onion and garlic; sauté until limp. Add peppers, tomato, herbs, and seasonings; reduce heat to simmer. Cook for 20 minutes. Add 1 cup beans and liquid to sauce. Mash well. Add this mixture to pot of beans; cook 20 minutes more.

Serve beans hot in bowls; top with chopped onions. Makes 6 servings.

Note: If you have a slow cooker, the beans can be cooked in it all day. Be sure to add water occasionally so that they don't boil dry.

refried beans
frijoles refritos

1 pound pinto beans
½ pound lean bacon (plus bacon grease)
1 medium onion, chopped
1 clove garlic, chopped (or 1 teaspoon garlic salt)
Shredded cheese for topping (optional)

Soak beans overnight.

Next day simmer beans 2 to 3 hours, until beans are soft, adding water as necessary to keep beans from boiling dry. Drain, saving liquid. Mash beans with potato masher or mixer.

Dice and fry bacon, onion, and garlic. Add mashed beans; fry until everything is well-mixed. If additional liquid is necessary, add some of liquid drained from beans.

Serve beans hot. Top with shredded cheese if desired. Makes 3 to 4 cups beans.

banana squash with brown sugar
calabaza enmielada con piloncillo

3 pounds banana squash or pumpkin
¼ cup brown sugar
3 tablespoons butter
½ teaspoon cinnamon

Pare squash or pumpkin; cut into 2-inch cubes. Cook in boiling salted water until tender. Drain well. Add brown sugar, butter, and cinnamon. Cook over low heat until butter melts and sugar softens. Stir to combine well. Serve squash hot. Makes 4 servings.

baked summer squash with cheese
calbacitas con queso al horno

1 pound (2 medium) summer squash
2 California green chilies, seeded and chopped
1½ cups grated Jack cheese
2 eggs, beaten
1 small can evaporated milk (5⅓ ounces)

Salt and pepper to taste
Paprika
1 tablespoon butter or margarine
2 tablespoons chopped onion

Slice summer squash in ½-inch slices. Parboil in boiling salted water until just tender. Drain.

Grease a 2-quart casserole. Place squash, chilies, and grated Jack cheese into casserole; toss gently to combine well.

Beat eggs, milk, salt, and pepper together. Pour over squash. Sprinkle with paprika.

Melt butter in small skillet; sauté onion until limp. Sprinkle onion and butter on top of casserole. Bake at 350°F for 40 minutes or until set. Makes 4 servings.

fried potatoes
papas fritos

4 medium potatoes
¼ cup lard
2 tablespoons achiote pips
1 medium onion, diced
Salt

Boil potatoes in their jackets until just tender. Drain and cool.

Meanwhile, heat lard in small, heavy saucepan until melted. Add achiote; cook over low heat 15 minutes or until lard is very orange in color. Cool; strain.

Peel and dice potatoes.

Heat colored lard in heavy skillet over medium heat until hot. Add potatoes and onion; fry until well-browned, stirring occasionally. Drain on absorbent paper, salt to taste, and serve. Makes 4 servings.

mexican corn
maíz mexicano

2 tablespoons vegetable oil
½ cup chopped green pepper
¼ cup chopped red pepper
½ fresh hot pepper, finely minced
1 16½-ounce can whole-kernel corn, drained

½ cup chopped well-drained canned tomatoes
½ teaspoon salt
¼ teaspoon pepper

Heat oil in medium saucepan. Sauté the peppers over medium heat 5 minutes. Add corn, tomatoes, salt, and pepper; heat through.

Serve corn hot as an accompaniment. Makes 4 servings.

fried spinach and onions
espinaca y cebollas fria

4 tablespoons bacon drippings
  or lard
1 large onion, sliced (1 cup)
1¼ pounds fresh spinach
  leaves, washed, trimmed,
  and stems removed

Salt and pepper to taste
⅛ teaspoon finely crushed
  dried red chilies (optional)

Melt lard or bacon drippings in large, heavy kettle over medium-high heat. Add onion; fry, stirring frequently, until lightly browned. Add spinach; cook, tossing constantly, 3 to 5 minutes, until wilted and coated with drippings. Season with salt, pepper, and powdered chilies to taste. Makes 4 servings.

zucchini with corn and peppers
calabacitas con maíz y chiles

2½ pounds zucchini
3 ears corn on the cob
1 medium green or red
  pepper, chopped
1 medium onion, chopped

2 cloves garlic, minced or
  pressed
3 tablespoons bacon drippings
  or melted butter
Salt and pepper to taste

Scrub zucchini and dice into bite-size pieces.

Cut corn off cob.

Combine zucchini, corn, pepper, onion, and garlic in frypan with butter. Cook, stirring often, until vegetables are tender-crisp, about 5 minutes. Add salt and pepper to taste.

Serve zucchini hot. Makes 8 to 10 servings.

zucchini fritters
tortas de calabacitas

¾ cup all-purpose flour, sifted
¾ teaspoon baking powder
½ teaspoon salt
1 cup grated zucchini squash
1 egg, slightly beaten
2 tablespoons milk

Sift together flour, baking powder, and salt.

In mixing bowl toss together flour mixture and grated zucchini.

Beat together egg and milk. Stir egg mixture into flour mixture.

Meanwhile, in deep fryer heat oil at least 1-inch deep to 360°F. Fry heaping tablespoons of batter until golden brown, turning occasionally. Drain on paper towels.

Serve fritters hot. Makes 3 to 4 servings (9 fritters).

breads, desserts, and sweets

corn tortillas
tortillas de maíz

2 cups instant Masa Harina
1 teaspoon salt
1¼ cups water

Combine Masa and salt in mixing bowl. Make a well in center; stir in water. Dough must be stiff enough to hold together, and not sticky. Add a little more water if necessary. Knead dough until pliable. Form into a 12-inch log; cut into 1-inch pieces. Roll pieces into balls; cover with a damp cloth while shaping tortillas.

shaping with a tortilla press
Place dough between 2 polyethylene bags, center on the press, and flatten. Carefully peel off plastic bags; stack tortillas between sheets of waxed paper until all are ready to cook.

without a tortilla press
Place dough ball between sheets of waxed paper; flatten with heavy skillet or large pie plate (and a lot of energy), or use a rolling pin. Turn tortilla to keep it round as you roll. Tortillas should be 6 inches in diameter and quite thin.

Heat a griddle or cast-iron skillet (ungreased) until quite hot.

Peel waxed paper off top of tortilla; place it on griddle. Wait several seconds, then gently peel waxed paper off other side of tortilla as the first side cooks on the griddle. Bake until lightly flecked with brown (about 2 minutes). Turn; cook 1 minute more. Stack, wrap in foil, and keep tortillas warm in oven. Makes 12 6-inch tortillas.

coconut flan
flan de coco

1 cup sugar
2 tablespoons water
4 eggs
1 14-ounce can sweetened
   condensed milk
1 cup water
1 teaspoon vanilla extract
½ cup flaked coconut

Combine sugar and 2 tablespoons water in small heavy skillet. Cook, stirring constantly, until caramelized and syrupy. Immediately pour into warm 3- to 4-cup buttered mold or casserole; tilt to coat bottom and sides of container while sugar is still hot.

Beat eggs well in medium mixing bowl. Add condensed milk, water, and flavoring; mix well. Pour into prepared mold or casserole; sprinkle with coconut.

Place casserole in a larger pan containing hot water to the level of the custard. Bake at 350°F for 1 hour or until a knife inserted in center of custard comes out clean. Cool mold completely. Loosen custard with a knife; invert on serving platter.

Serve with the caramel spooned over each serving. Makes 6 servings.

mexican trifle
postre de virrey

¼ cup sugar
1 tablespoon cornstarch
¼ teaspoon salt
2 cups milk
2 eggs, slightly beaten
1 teaspoon vanilla
4 cups cubed pound cake
4 tablespoons brandy
4 tablespoons apricot
   preserves
½ cup whipped cream
1 tablespoon confectioners'
   sugar
Grated semisweet chocolate
Toasted slivered almonds

Combine sugar, cornstarch, and salt in medium saucepan. Stir in milk until well-blended. Cook over medium heat, stirring constantly, until mixture boils (it will be quite thin).

Add a little custard to beaten eggs; beat well. Return to saucepan; cook, stirring constantly, until mixture starts to bubble. Stir in vanilla; cool, covered with waxed paper.

Place cake cubes in glass bowl. Sprinkle with 3 tablespoons of the brandy, and drizzle with preserves. Pour custard over cake cubes.

Whip the cream with confectioners' sugar until stiff. Fold in 1 tablespoon brandy.

Top the cake and custard with whipped cream. Garnish with grated chocolate and almonds. Cover and chill for several hours before serving. Makes 4 to 6 servings.

mexican cinnamon tea cakes
polvorones de canela

1 cup butter
1½ cups sugar
2 eggs
2¾ cups flour
1 teaspoon cream of tartar
¼ teaspoon salt
1 teaspoon baking powder
2 tablespoons sugar
2 teaspoons cinnamon

Cream butter and 1½ cups sugar. Add eggs.

Sift dry ingredients; add to egg mixture.

Shape dough into small balls, using approximately 1 teaspoon dough for each cookie.

Roll balls in mixture of 2 tablespoons sugar and 2 teaspoons cinnamon. Flatten slightly. Place on greased cookie sheet. Bake for 8 to 10 minutes at 400°F. Remove from cookie sheet and cool on a rack. Makes 4 dozen.

fried crullers
churros

Oil for deep frying
½ lime
1 slice white bread, cut into cubes
1 cup water
1 10-ounce package pie-crust mix
3 eggs
Confectioners' sugar

In large, heavy saucepan heat oil with lime and bread slice to 370°F. Oil should be at least 3 inches deep and pan no more than half full.

Bring water to a boil in medium saucepan. Quickly stir pie-crust mix into boiling water; continue stirring until mixture forms a ball and leaves sides of pan. Remove from heat. Beat in eggs, one at a time, beating well after each addition.

Remove bread and lime half from oil when bread is golden brown.

Transfer dough mixture to pastry bag fitted with star tip. Squeeze dough into hot fat in a continuous spiral to fill pan without crowding; cook until well-browned. Drain on absorbent paper, dust with confectioners' sugar, and break into pieces to serve. Continue until all dough is used.

Serve crullers immediately with coffee. Makes about 12 6-inch pieces.

sweet fritters
bunnelos

4¾ cups flour
½ cup sugar
¼ teaspoon salt
1 cup water
2 eggs
3 tablespoons rum
Oil for frying
1 teaspoon ground cinnamon
½ cup sugar

Sift flour, sugar, and salt together into large bowl.

Beat water, eggs, and rum together. Pour into flour mixture; mix to form a stiff dough. Turn out on floured board; knead for 2 minutes or until smooth. Cut into 4 pieces. Roll each piece on floured pastry cloth to a rectangle (10 × 15 inches); cut into strips (2 × 5 inches). Shape by twisting 2 strips together, or cut a 1-inch slit down center of strip and pull 1 end through slit.

Heat oil to 370°F in an electric skillet.

Meanwhile, combine cinnamon and sugar in shallow pan.

Deep-fry pastries until golden. Drain briefly, dip in cinnamon and sugar, and coat well. Makes 40.

puffed bread
sopaipillas

Delicious for breakfast, lunch, or dinner. May be served as a hot bread or with soup or guacamole.

4 cups flour
4 teaspoons baking powder
2 teaspoons salt

¼ cup shortening
1 to 1½ cups water, as needed
Oil for frying

Sift dry ingredients into mixing bowl. Cut in shortening. Add water, a little at a time, stirring to form a stiff dough. Knead until smooth. Roll thin; cut into 2-inch squares or triangles.

Heat oil in deep, heavy pan to 365°F; deep fry dough pieces a few at a time until golden brown. They will puff up as they fry.

Serve Puffed Bread hot with butter and jelly or honey. Makes about 40.

flour tortillas
tortillas de harina

2 cups unsifted all-purpose
    flour
1 teaspoon salt
¼ cup lard
½ cup water

Combine flour and salt in mixing bowl. Work lard into flour mixture with your fingers until mixture resembles coarse cornmeal. Make a well in center of flour mixture. Add water; stir to combine. Form into a ball. If mixture is dry, add a little more water. Knead for 3 minutes on a floured board. Divide into 6 balls. Cover; let rest 20 minutes.

Roll each ball on a floured pastry cloth to a 7- to 8-inch circle; trim, if necessary, using a dinner plate as a guide. Stack tortillas between sheets of waxed paper until all are rolled. Bake on an ungreased, moderately hot griddle until edges dry and brown flecks appear (2 minutes). Turn; bake 1 minute more. Wrap tortillas in foil and keep them warm until all are cooked. Makes 6 7- to 8-inch tortillas.

glazed fruit bread
pan dulce de frutas

batter
⅔ cup raisins
⅔ cup candied fruit
¼ cup rum
1 cup butter
1 cup sugar
4 eggs
2¾ cups all-purpose flour
1 teaspoon double-acting baking powder

glaze
1¼ cups confectioners' sugar
3½ tablespoons rum

Combine raisins and candied fruit in small bowl; toss with rum. Set aside.

Cream butter and sugar until light. Add eggs one at a time; beat well after each addition.

Sift flour and baking powder together. Add flour mixture to egg mixture; mix to combine. Fold mixed fruits into batter. Pour mixture into greased 11 × 7 × 1¾-inch baking pan; bake at 350°F for 40 to 50 minutes or until a toothpick inserted in center of cake comes out clean. Cool.

Combine confectioners' sugar and rum; stir to form a smooth icing. Ice cooled cake; allow icing to dry before cutting.

Cut into small squares and serve with coffee or chocolate. Makes 1 large loaf, 11 × 7 × 1¾ (about 12 pieces).

king's bread ring
rosca de reyes

King's Bread is served on Twelfth Night. The lucky (?) one who gets the coin in the bread must give a party on February 2, which is El Dia de la Candelaria (The Day of the Candle Mass).

1 teaspoon dried orange peel
2 tablespoons rum
2 packages active dry yeast
½ cup warm water
½ cup milk, scalded
⅓ cup sugar

⅓ cup shortening
2 teaspoons salt
4 cups all-purpose flour
3 eggs, well-beaten
Melted butter or margarine

topping
Candied cherries, cut into
   small pieces
Candied orange peel, in strips

Soak dried orange peel in rum.

To make bread, soften yeast in warm water.

Pour hot milk over sugar, shortening, and salt in large bowl, stirring until sugar is dissolved and shortening is melted. Cool to lukewarm. Beat in 1 cup flour, then the eggs and softened yeast, and the rum-soaked orange peel. Add enough flour to make a stiff dough.

Turn dough onto a floured surface; knead until smooth and satiny. Roll dough into a long rope; shape into a ring, sealing the ends together. Transfer to greased cookie sheet. Push a coin into the dough so it is completely covered. Brush with melted butter. Cover with a towel; let rise until double in bulk (about 1½ hours). Bake at 375°F for 25 to 30 minutes or until golden brown. Cool on wire rack.

When cool, frost bread ring with Confectioners' Icing, and decorate with candied cherries and orange-peel strips. Makes 1 large ring of bread.

confectioners' sugar icing
1⅓ cups confectioners' sugar
4 teaspoons water
½ teaspoon vanilla

In a small bowl combine confectioners' sugar, water, and vanilla until smooth.

mocha cherry and nut cookies
galletas de mocha y cereza y nuez

1 cup butter
½ cup sugar
2 teaspoons vanilla
2 cups sifted flour
¼ cup unsweetened cocoa
1 tablespoon instant coffee

½ teaspoon salt
1 cup finely chopped pecans
½ cup chopped maraschino
   cherries
1 box confectioners' sugar

Cream butter, sugar, and vanilla until fluffy.

Sift together flour, cocoa, instant coffee, and salt. Gradually add dry ingredients to creamed mixture. Add pecans and cherries. Chill dough.

Shape dough into balls, using 1 generous teaspoon of dough for each ball. Place on greased cookie sheets. Bake in 325°F oven 20 minutes. Remove from cookie sheets to cooling racks. While warm, sprinkle with confectioners' sugar. Makes 6 dozen.

cream-cheese pastry with sweet potato, pineapple, and coconut filling or prune filling
empanadas de dulce

cream-cheese pastry

(Prepare and chill at least 6 hours ahead.)

1 cup butter	2 cups flour
1 8-ounce package cream cheese	½ teaspoon salt

Cream butter and cream cheese until smooth. Work in flour and salt until blended. Chill in airtight container at least 6 hours.

sweet potato, pineapple, and coconut filling

1 cup mashed sweet potatoes	½ teaspoon cinnamon
1 cup drained crushed pineapple	¾ cup flaked or shredded coconut
½ cup sugar	

Mix potatoes, pineapple, sugar, cinnamon, and coconut in saucepan. Cook over low heat, stirring constantly, until mixture thickens, about 5 to 10 minutes. Cool thoroughly.

prune filling

8 ounces prunes, pitted	½ teaspoon cinnamon
⅓ cup sugar	Dash of nutmeg

Cover prunes with water; boil for 20 minutes or until tender. Puree the prunes. Stir in sugar, cinnamon, and nutmeg. Simmer, stirring, over low heat for 5 minutes. Cool. Makes 1 cup.

Divide cream-cheese pastry in half. Prepare on lightly floured surface. Roll dough until ⅛ inch thick. Cut into 3-inch rounds.

Place 1 teaspoon filling in center of each round. Moisten edges with water; fold pastry over filling to form a half-moon turnover. Press lightly to seal; crimp edges. Bake on ungreased sheets at 375°F for 18 to 20 minutes. When crisp and golden, remove from oven; place on racks to cool.

Empanadas may be dipped in a cinnamon and sugar mixture while warm. Makes 32.

Note: Each batch of filling is enough for one pastry recipe plus extra, which may be served with meat or fowl as a side dish.

green tomato pie
pastel de tomate verde

6 to 8 medium green tomatoes, peeled and sliced	2 tablespoons butter
1 lemon, thinly sliced	½ teaspoon ground cinnamon
2 tablespoons cornstarch	¼ teaspoon salt
2 tablespoons water	1 frozen pie shell and frozen top crust or pie-crust mix
1 cup sugar	

Boil tomatoes and lemon, then cover and simmer 10 minutes, until tomatoes appear transparent.

Combine cornstarch and water; add to tomato mixture. Add sugar, butter, cinnamon, and salt. Stirring constantly, bring to a boil; continue boiling for 1 minute. Remove from heat.

Follow pastry instructions for baking a two-crust pie. Place filling in pie, add top crust, seal, flute edges, and cut steam vents in top crust. Bake at 425°F approximately 35 minutes.

This is best served at room temperature. Makes 8 servings.

broiled fruit with cinnamon
frutas con canela

3 bananas
½ medium pineapple (or 3 slices canned pineapple)
2 medium apples
½ cup melted butter
½ cup brown sugar
Ground cinnamon

Peel bananas.

Peel pineapple; remove core. Cut slices ¾ inch thick.

Peel and core apples; slice ¾ inch thick.

Place fruits on cookie sheet lined with foil. Brush well with melted butter. Sprinkle with brown sugar and cinnamon. Broil 3 to 4 inches from heat 5 minutes, turning once.

Serve with sour cream or softened vanilla ice cream, flavored with rum. Makes 4 to 6 servings.

coffee dessert
postre de cafe

1¼ cups water
¼ cup sugar
2 cloves
1 strip orange peel
1 strip lemon peel
1 small piece cinnamon stick
2 teaspoons instant-coffee powder
1 envelope unflavored gelatin
¼ cup coffee liquer
Whipped cream or whipped topping

In small saucepan combine water, sugar, cloves, orange peel, lemon peel, and cinnamon stick. Bring to a boil; boil for 2 minutes. Strain; add coffee powder.

Soften gelatin in coffee liquer. Add hot coffee mixture to gelatin; stir until gelatin is dissolved. Pour into 3 or 4 small molds, rinsed with cold water. Chill overnight.

Unmold at serving time by dipping in hot water. Top with whipped cream or whipped topping. Makes 3 to 4 servings.

mocha parfait

2 bananas
Juice of 1 lemon (2 tablespoons)
16 walnut halves
½ cup cold heavy whipping cream
½ teaspoon vanilla
2 tablespoons sugar
1½ pints coffee ice cream
Bitter chocolate curls

Peel bananas, slice, and dip slices in lemon juice. Divide bananas among 4 parfait glasses. Top each with 4 walnut halves. Chill the glasses while whipping the cream.

Pour whipping cream into small mixing bowl. Add vanilla; whip until stiff, gradually adding sugar while whipping.

At serving time, cube the ice cream; divide it among prepared parfait glasses. Top with whipped cream and chocolate curls. Makes 4 servings.

gelatin dessert
almendrada

1 tablespoon (1 envelope)
  unflavored gelatin
½ cup cold pineapple juice
4 egg whites
¼ teaspoon salt
¾ cup sugar
½ teaspoon vanilla
¼ teaspoon almond extract

2 tablespoons chopped
  maraschino cherries
¼ cup crushed pineapple
⅓ cup chopped blanched
  almonds
Red and green food coloring
  as needed

Soften gelatin in cold pineapple juice. Dissolve over hot water.

Beat egg whites until foamy, add salt and sugar gradually, and continue beating until soft-peak stage is reached. Add dissolved gelatin to egg whites; beat until thick and of a marshmallow consistency. Add vanilla and almond extract. Divide into 3 parts; color 1 part pink, and add the maraschino cherries; color 1 part green and add pineapple; add chopped almonds to remainder. Mold in oblong loaf pan, 9½ × 5¼ × 2¾ inches, putting white layer on bottom, then green, then pink, to represent Mexican flag colors. Small individual glass serving cups may be used instead of loaf pan. Let stand until set.

Cut in slices; garnish with whipped cream, or serve with a custard sauce. Makes 8 servings.

hot chocolate mexican-style
chocolate

hot chocolate mexican-style

Traditional Mexican chocolate is beaten with a *molinillo* before serving. An egg beater and a lot of energy make a good substitute!

2 1-ounce squares
  unsweetened chocolate
½ teaspoon vanilla
1 teaspoon ground cinnamon
4 tablespoons heavy cream
2 cups milk
2 egg yolks
2 tablespoons sugar
3 ounces brandy
4 cinnamon sticks

In a saucepan combine chocolate, vanilla, cinnamon, and cream; place over very low heat, stirring until chocolate is melted. Add milk slowly to chocolate mixture; mix well. Warm over very low heat. Do not allow mixture to boil.

Beat egg yolks and sugar until foamy. Slowly pour part of chocolate mixture into egg yolks, beating well.

Pour egg-yolk mixture back into saucepan; beat. Add brandy to chocolate mixture; beat until mixture is frothy. Serve hot chocolate immediately in small cups with cinnamon sticks used as stirrers. Makes 4 servings.

Note: A simpler method for making delicious chocolate is as follows: For each cup of chocolate, heat 1 cup milk until quite hot (do not boil). Pour over 1 ounce (per cup of milk) of grated Mexican chocolate; stir until melted. Whip with a rotary beater until frothy, and serve. If Mexican chocolate is unavailable, substitute 1 ounce of unsweetened chocolate, grated, and ¼ teaspoon ground cinnamon for each ounce of Mexican chocolate.

index